Let

THEM
LEAD

*How to
Command
Less and
Accomplish
More*

MICHAELA M. HART

PRESIDENT & CEO, MICHAELA, INC.

LET THEM LEAD

How to Command Less and Accomplish More

ISBN 978-1-61961-366-9

LIONCREST
PUBLISHING

For my father, Mr. Frederick R. Hart III—for giving me more of him than he ever gave himself, including his absolutely perfect last name! I love you Daddy-O! XO XO

PRAISE FOR *LET THEM LEAD*

"This book rocks! Right from the get-go, full of personal and practical information to help everyone navigate organizational waters effectively. You feel like Michaela is looking directly into your eyes and heart, caring deeply about your success and welfare, and sharing her sage advice and perspective.

There's no B.S. here—packed with practical insights, as well as an abiding care and respect for the reader. This book is too good to be true, but it is true. Michaela is like that mythical leader who takes you aside, dispensing practical wisdom and experiential secrets.

This volume has the keys to the treasure chest for making the most of organizational life, and it has practical insights whether you are just starting your career or have been doing your corporate thing for decades."

– BARRY Z. POSNER, PHD, ACCOLTI ENDOWED PROFESSOR OF LEADERSHIP, SANTA CLARA UNIVERSITYDEAN (1997-2009), LEAVEY SCHOOL OF BUSINESS, SANTA CLARA UNIVERSITY, CO-AUTHOR: THE LEADERSHIP CHALLENGE AND THE TRUTH ABOUT LEADERSHIP

"*Let Them Lead captures the essence of Michaela's belief system and her passion to get everyone to follow their heart to happiness. Practical and accessible concepts easily applied by anyone. A universe unfolding companion for the left-brained. A must read.*"

– TONY LEE, CHIEF OF WETWARE, TONY INC.

"*Michaela is a force of nature. She takes the bull by the horns and gets the job done. Not only has she added 'author' to her resume, but this book knocks it out of the park. As an MBA graduate, I've read my share of leadership books, and Let Them Lead rivals the best. I couldn't put it down, not because she's my friend of 30+ years, but because she takes all that is Michaela, unique, bold, caring, fearless, and unabashedly honest, and puts it into 182 pages to show how to make any employee shine, regardless of their unique strengths. Imagine a better and more productive workplace where Michaela-channeling bosses actually empower their employees and quite simply just 'let them lead.' Well done, woman, well done!*"

– MARY BETH WHITCOMB, DVM MBA; ASSOCIATE PROFESSOR, SCHOOL OF VETERINARY MEDICINE, UNIVERSITY OF CALIFORNIA, DAVIS

"*This book is a practical recipe to empower and inspire a team. Michaela has taken her own proven techniques and learning and put them in a very accessible format for all of us to utilize. The advice and practices she offers will help improve our leadership and our work environment. This book has the potential to change lives and deliver joy.*"

– ADAM BERLEW, PRESIDENT AND CEO OF ADAM INC. AND VP CUSTOMER ENGAGEMENT MARKETING, BROCADE, INC.

"I have worked with Michaela for many years. She demonstrates insightful diplomacy, creative organizational abilities, and effective communication skills that ensure that the needs of her widespread professional network are more than suitably addressed. Michaela has a deeply engrained sense of integrity and an unwavering sense of urgency, coupled with a relentlessly positive attitude and sense of humor. Michaela has a truly unique approach that works internationally too!"

– HERMANN LEHN, PHD, CONSULTANT AND FOUNDER OF LEHNCONSULTING, LEVERKUSEN, GERMANY

"If my mom was an app, you would most definitely want to download her. In Let Them Lead, she has downloaded herself for you!"

– NIKYRA R. ADAMS, HBIC OF NIKKI INC. AND UC BERKELEY STUDENT

"It's hard not to get caught up in the whirlwind of Michaela's ideas! Her real world examples have a radical practicality—turning today's Command-and-Control management style on its head to breed positive energy, productivity, and employee retention. This isn't just another book on being a better manager; it's a book about becoming a better YOU (as a manager or not!). It will teach you to think like a Rock Star, speak with your feet, create 1+1=10 relationships, and intention success (for you AND your team)! I've not only read these philosophies, I've lived them, and they really do work!"

– ROBERT FRINK, DIRECTOR OF VISION & LONG-TERM STRATEGY, ROBERT FRINK, LLC

"Michaela has written a book that is not only warm and humorous but deeply insightful as well. Her experience, combined with the wisdom she's gained along her journey as a consultant and cheerleader, provides a reliable set of guideposts that anyone in leadership can use. You are the leader of your own life, and Michaela recognizes this profound truth and insists each person access their innate intuition to inform their life choices. As one who spends a great deal of time exploring the intersection of spirituality and leadership, I highly recommend this book. Taken to 'Hart', this book has the potential to transform your entire life."

– REV. KAREN EPPS, FOUNDER UNITY GLOBAL HEART MINISTRY, LEADERSHIP DEVELOPMENT FACILITATOR, MOTIVATIONAL SPEAKER, SQ21 CERTIFIED COACH, AND INTEGRAL PRACTITIONER

CONTENTS

FOREWORD

JUST LIKE MICHAELA IS NOT YOUR AVERAGE, ORDINARY
Quality and Regulatory professional (by any means), this
is not your average, ordinary book about leadership. What
began with me hiring her a number of years ago to help
build a very special start-up molecular diagnostics company,
culminated recently in an email exchange that ended with
two very simple and heartfelt words: "Love you!" Yes, those
words were spoken between professional colleagues.

For as you will read and learn here, the workplace does not
have to subscribe to the old Command-and-Control leadership style. It's quite possible to wake up every morning and
genuinely *want* to come to work. And likewise, it's also possible to work a happy, reasonable workday amongst caring
co-workers before heading home to what really matters, i.e.,
your home life, and most importantly, to YOU!

While Silicon Valley may have provided the perfect backdrop for a new way of thinking, Michaela brought us a new way of leading. We were all witnesses to Michaela's M-powered "teach them to lead themselves first" style that you, too, are about to be bathed in. You are going to learn that in order to lead anyone or anything else, you need to be leading yourself first. And after you have your own self in order, she's going to help you understand how to lead others.

While Michaela may have moved on to another company, there's a little piece of her heart that still lies right here with us, and she will be quick to tell you that there's still a little bit of us within her heart as well. That's the kind of relationship that she's going to teach you how to create—at work, of all places.

And I have to be honest, as the President and CEO, it was all relatively easy on my end; I simply *let her lead*!

— BONNIE ANDERSON, PRESIDENT AND CEO, VERACYTE, INC.

PROLOGUE

THIS BOOK WAS INSPIRED BY AND WRITTEN FOR TWO very special people in my life, Ambika and Thanda. These two individuals have been my inspirational bookends; they are the yin and the yang of this book. You will learn about Ambika here now and about Thanda at this book's end.

A few years back, I was at a company supporting the turn-around of a department that I projected would take about a year; it later turned into two years, because these situations are always a lot more complicated than they first seem. The funny thing about my job is that my goal is to essentially put myself out of business. I teach people leadership skills with the intention that ultimately, they will be functioning so well, they won't need me to lead them anymore—they will have essentially learned how to lead themselves. As strange as this may sound, when it's complete and time for me to leave, it means that I have successfully worked myself out of a job and am ready for the next adventure; this is true success to me.

As my departure time was nearing at this particular company, one of the things that the staff and I had been working on was the practice of bringing solutions, rather than problems, to the table in the face of an issue. I try to ingrain this mindset in the employees who I work with from day one. The last thing I ever want to hear from them are problems without possible solutions! They are the ones in the trenches, they are doing the work, and they should be able to come up with viable, actionable solutions for every single one of their own problems. Right?

When I first met Ambika, she was a shy girl and her confidence was almost non-existent, but over the course of our time together, she had emerged as a natural leader. She had risen from probably the lowest woman on the totem pole to the leader of the entire department. She is currently the lab manager, and I could not be more proud of how far she has risen in such a short time. Ambika scheduled an Outlook calendar appointment to come see me, and she let me know in advance that she had formulated a solution, which we both knew really meant that she had a problem. See how that works?

Ambika arrived at my office and announced point-blank that she wanted me to write a book. Her reasoning was that the team was very close to being ready to lead themselves, which was true, but they weren't quite ready to let go of me, live in the flesh, every day yet. She wanted me to capture all of the stories that I had shared with them over the course of the previous two years. She argued that I could very easily sit in my office and pretend to be working, when in fact I would actually be writing this book. :) That way, they would get to keep me for a little bit longer, and in the end, they would have a book with all of my stories in it. Her timing was fortuitous because little did she, or anyone else, know that I was in the middle of interviewing for another position at a new company. Needless to say, I was deeply touched. With that "solution," and in that moment, Ambika had intentioned this book's inception.

Not long after my conversation with Ambika, I was driving to work, stuck in Bay Area traffic, and Chris Daughtry's song "Waiting for Superman" came on the radio. This song was relatively new, but it's basically the same message as Bon Jovi's "Superman Tonight" song from a number of years ago. They are both about waiting for someone to save you, the stereotype of women being rescued, the damsel in distress scene, etc. The whole concept of being "rescued" annoys the self-made girl in me to no end, but I am a Bon Jovi fan and the Daughtry song was written in a similar vein. And then, all of a sudden, I thought about these songs a little deeper and asked myself, "Am I waiting for a superman?" No, thankfully, I'm really not, but I wanted to get to the heart of why these songs were touching me so.

You see, I have learned to go deep, to look underneath the surface of problems and find the solutions. I approached this song the same way that I would treat any other problem. I realized that I was not waiting for a superman at all, but what, in fact, I was waiting for was my very own superwoman song. Why hadn't that been written? And for that matter, why haven't many superwoman songs been written in general?

In about ten minutes, I composed it in my head. Yes, I wrote my very own superwoman song. Now, keep in mind that I have never played a musical instrument nor can I sing; the closest that I have ever come is writing a few poems. But I opened up my heart and my soul and my mind, and as soon as I got to work, I transcribed the song in my head into a Word document on my computer. A friend of mine had it produced a few weeks later for my birthday, and my employees at work posted it on YouTube. It's called "S of Chalk."[1] This song explains a lot about me, my "kids," and my companies.

This song represents exactly what I teach. If you want your own song, write it! Is something standing in your way? Move it. Do you feel stuck or trapped? Make a choice to stick it out and make it work, or take a hike and find something better. Gossip and complaining never solved a single problem; pointing a finger at someone else simply leaves three fingers pointing back at you. You are your own best cheerleader, and you have the power to influence your own future. Every single minute is a choice, and every situation is an opportunity.

Ambika's "solution" came back to me tenfold. If I can write a song in just a morning, then I should be able to write a book. This book is my gift for her, and Thanda, and for all of the "kids" in my life—you know who you are—thank you for touching my heart and for inspiring these pages. May you also allow these words to touch you, the reader.

1   https://www.youtube.com/watch?v=tOSxdztc5ts

INTRODUCTION

"A good leader inspires others with confidence in her; a
great leader inspires them with confidence in themselves."

– ANONYMOUS

BUILDING QUALITY IN

The appropriate term for what I do professionally is lead
quality and regulatory departments. I am initially hired
to identify the gaps (or problems) in an organization and
implement a turnaround plan for improved compliance,
productivity, and profitability. I go into biotechnology or
pharmaceutical organizations and perform a series of audits
that pinpoint the issues. Once the problems and proposed
solutions have been shared with management, I stay on to
oversee the operational cleanup as well. Most often, it's the
people, not the processes, with the widest "gap."

Not surprisingly, finding people who can successfully lead other people (in any setting) is not an easy task. I typically wind up with a company for double the length of time of the original contract because of the unforeseen implementation pieces. A complete turnaround can take anywhere from one to five years, depending on the size of the company and the depth of their problems. I partner directly with Human Resources (HR), and just about everyone else for that matter. Together, we build quality into the organization and give the staff the tools they need to be sustainable. This isn't a "bolt-on" scenario; bolt-ons are fake and almost always require significant, additional, downstream repair jobs.

My intention in the chapters that follow here is to share with you my bag of tricks, or the tools of my "M-trade." I have learned these lessons over the course of many years, and I would love for everyone to feel empowered enough to lead themselves through the sometimes murky career waters and to emerge on the other side where they can live and love the lives they were meant to live at work to the absolute fullest. Ambika and the rest of my work "kids" think that these stories and strategies have lasting value, and I'm hopeful that you will too.

COMMAND AND CONTROL

The typical management style is one that we can all recognize because it is still the norm today; it's hierarchical and militaristic by nature. The bosses hold all of the power and use it to, well, boss everyone around. Oftentimes, the only difference between you and your boss is the information that he or she has access to, and they keep this information close to the chest; they don't share it with anyone around them. Essentially, they're not giving much of anything. In fact, what they are doing is taking, i.e., taking energy, motivation, and the desire to succeed away from everyone else around them in their organization. Sound familiar?

On the flip side, there are management movements going on around the country and the world that promote "No Management Management." Others might call it "chaos" or "anarchy." The fact is, there needs to be some degree of order, or corporate America would look like *Lord of the Flies*. We are all mammals, and mammals can have a tendency to tear each other to shreds out there in the wilderness. There needs to be some semblance of structure, or the animals will literally be running the zoo. So, where is the middle ground in all of this?

The workforce is changing, whether the controlling bosses like it or not. The generations of the future are not going to tolerate Command-and-Control leadership for long; this has already been proven. In fact, just working with and being around Millennials recently has been an eye-opening experience. They have given me an education in the speed of learning through their seemingly endless access to information. If you present them with a problem or a question, nothing stops them from immediately going to their phones or tablets and finding the Internet's answers. It's not even a hunger for knowledge; it's their Millennially-coded, default instinct. Good for them; the rest of us should pay attention!

All the Millennials need is just the smallest, teensiest bit of direction, and off they go. They have YouTube, they instantly download books via their Kindle app, they Skype each other, they join meet ups, and they speak with strangers around the world about ideas. They have immediate access to communication and information, which combined is a force of staggering proportions. They don't care that they aren't going to own a house tomorrow; that's not what drives them. They want to have fun at work. Quality of life is paramount for them. Therefore, the Command-and-Control structure is never going to work with them. They're quick to "speak with their feet" and high tail it out the front door, regardless of the size of your corporation or their unvested stock option balance.

I've looked far and wide in an attempt to "reference" or ground what I do with organizational models that exist in the business world. The one that matches pretty closely is the Sustainable Performance Model.[2] Essentially, the four components are the people, the product, the culture, and the environment. A functioning work environment is one in which information is shared, incivility is minimized, and people are empowered to do their jobs through decision-making power and behavioral accountability. Add some legitimate "heart" to this model and you might get close to what I inspire.

---

2   *Creating Sustainable Performance*, Gretchen Sprietzer and *Harvard Business Review*, Jan-Feb 2012

Regardless of demographics, my M-camp curriculum and management style is the same for everyone at all levels within a company, from my admins to my senior management. It all starts with creating a safe environment for my employees to excel in, i.e., an environment where they feel comfortable and confident to express their ideas, make mistakes, and genuinely learn.

To give you an example, I'm working with someone now who is brand new to management. I know that his motivations run deeper than simply a higher salary, but if you want to make more money, oftentimes you need to have more responsibility. The only trouble is that this person has never managed anyone in his life before, nor has he taken a single class on this subject. Although, he has led his young son's soccer teams, and that's a very good start!

At first, we brainstormed ideas on how he could get some practice safely. He wanted me to hire someone and have that person report to him, but that would have been way too risky; if his hire was problematic in any way (and chances are high that he or she would be, think Murphy's Law here), this new manager would be a train wreck right out of the gate. He wouldn't be able to handle the person, and he would appear incompetent to management. We had to make this easy (and most importantly, safe) for him.

My suggestion was to bring in a summer intern for him; he would conduct the interviews, check the references, and do everything associated with making the hiring decision. The upside to this idea was that the intern would be free, and if the person turned out to be a total disaster, he or she would disappear in ninety days, and the company would have no idea that any of this had ever happened.

Slowly, he started to see the beauty of this logic. Even if this new manager bombed the experience, it wouldn't matter! But the fact is, he was not going to bomb because he had been set up for success. The fear of failure had been removed, and we had just created a safe environment for him. And thus, we set out to find a "starter employee" for him. Not coincidently, I paired him up with an employee who needed a "starter boss" (it was her first big corporation experience), and the two of them lived happily ever after all summer long.

This is one of the biggest problems in the workplace—most bosses set people up to fail. They don't take the time, or have the know-how or bandwidth, to even think about setting their employees up for success, and the repercussions of not doing this are huge. I can promise you that our summer school experiment was a lot cheaper and far more rewarding than sending this new manager to six weeks of "Welcome to Being a Boss" classes in another country halfway across the globe.

Even though this new manager was smart in many ways, he had a lot of fear and relatively zero experience with management. This is not uncommon.

Fear should be treated the same way at work that it's treated outside of work: by making the situation safe. If someone is afraid of heights, you put ten nets underneath them. You don't take them to the top of the highest building that you can find and watch them teeter. Give them the nets and watch them soar. And do you know how some firearms instructors teach students how to shoot perfect bull's eyes from day one? They begin with targets that are *very* close! Get it?

THE SECRET

People ask me how I became such a strong leader with an army of loyal fans. I've won a number of awards for leadership management, and I'm not going to wait until the end of the book, or even chapter one, to reveal my secret. It's so simple and so genuine that I am going to put it out here right now. *I care.* For real.

One of the most valuable things that I learned to do at a very young age is to show up in the moment and sincerely be there for the employee, their career, and the organization at large. I can literally remove my ego from my body, put it on a figurative shelf, and genuinely be present for that person in that moment. I honestly believe that this sole characteristic is what separates the successful leaders from the unsuccessful ones, i.e., you need to genuinely care about others.

My new manager is a perfect example of this. I wasn't initially thinking about the intern, or the budget, or myself, or even the company that hired both of us; I was genuinely thinking about him and what I knew in my heart would be the best path forward for him. He couldn't do it on his own.

This brand new manager couldn't just teach himself how to manage; he needed leadership and someone who cared enough about him to create a safe path for him to confidently walk down. And if there were political land mines in his way, then I needed to paint them white for him. That's leadership.

The following chapters hold an M-powered playbook to create an amazing, inspired, and self-motivated team. Ditch the evil boss in the ivory tower mentality and tap into what really resonates with employees, especially those from the up-and-coming generations. Employee engagement through self-leadership is the only way to foster independence and confidence. Go ahead, give them the tools, create a safe environment, and *let them lead*.

CHAPTER I

NOBODY CARES ABOUT YOU, EXCEPT FOR YOU

AS HARSH AS THIS MAY SOUND, THE TRUTH IS THAT nobody really cares about you as much as you care about yourself. If you find yourself disappointed by someone's behavior, ask yourself, "Why would they wash my face to make themselves look better?" Whenever I have a brand new student, employee, or manager come on board, I lead with this hard truth, not to scare them or come off sounding unfeeling, but to highlight that in order to succeed, they need to own their choices and decisions. This journey is about YOU. It's not about the company or about me; this truly is chapter one.

On the whole, people (sadly) do not normally think about putting themselves first. They take better care of their corporations and their cars than they do themselves. They sit around waiting for the rest of the world to happen to them: the perfect boss, the promotion, the new job, the superman. People don't realize that this is not how the universe works. Before you can assist anyone else, you need to put on your own oxygen mask first (just like the flight attendants tell you!).

Give this some thought and ask yourself, "Am I voting for myself first, every day?" How often do you suggest that you are the right person for the job, or that you should lead the team or the new project? How often are you watching other people put forth your idea and then get all of the credit for it? This has happened to almost everyone. You're sitting in a meeting, not saying anything, the guy next to you puts forth *your* idea (you know it's yours), and then he gets all the glory. You kick yourself silently under the table, "Why didn't I say anything?" Because you don't get it yet; nobody cares about you, except for you, buddy.

This mindset is about taking responsibility for your own life. I do not support the "woulda, coulda, shoulda" mentality and people who embrace the victim role in their life. You need to be able to wake up, look yourself in the mirror, and truly, genuinely like what you see there. I bought a sticker that says, "You Are the Fairest of Them All" for the antique mirror that hangs in my bedroom to remind myself of this every morning. I'm talking about self-love here, which is something that our society has a tendency to shun; when in fact, we should embrace it. Who else is going to do a better job of that than you?

If you don't care about yourself, then why should I, as your boss, care about you? Why should I spend any energy to teach or coach you from good to great? If nobody cares about you, *especially you*, then guess what? Nothing is going to happen! You will stay stuck, and you will keep blaming everyone else around you. You need to love yourself before you can ever care for anyone else at work. Learning to love yourself is not an easy task, but it's the most important first step to transform you into a leader of others. Think *critical path* here.

THE COLD HARD TRUTH 1A

I once had a boss who told me, right in the middle of my end-of-year performance evaluation, that if I was diagnosed with cancer tomorrow, he would not come visit me in the hospital. I was devastated. Why would he say something so cruel? I was practically crying. What a terrible person, right? Wrong. What he was trying to tell me was that I was working way too hard for him and our company.

This was an eye-opener. I was shocked, but it was at this moment that I began to understand a fundamental, although very sad and painful, truth. If you think that your boss genuinely cares about you as a person, then you are most likely dead wrong. In that moment, I asked myself, "*Who* am I doing this for? And *why* am I even doing it at all?"

You should not be working to make anyone else happy, your boss (especially) included. Working is a means to an end to finance the things that we genuinely enjoy, whether that is time with our families, a vacation, or anything else in life that requires our hard-earned dollars.

This philosophy sunk in a little deeper for me when I lived in Europe as an expat for a few years. Europeans understand this; just try getting anything done in July or August over there. They are all off on "holiday." In new organizations, you will frequently hear me ask, "We are all here to finance our personal lives, right?" Sadly, this is a new concept to most.

Whenever I launch into the "chapter one" lesson with my new staff, they are equally as taken aback as I was all of those years ago. They do a double take and say, "Wait. What? You don't care about me?" Well, the difference is that I do genuinely care about them, and they will learn that over time. But "m the exception as bosses go, not the rule. You need to understand this about yourself: it's your life, it's what you produce, it's your heart, and it's your path. Stop expecting anybody else to pave it for you.

The man who taught me this important lesson, unwittingly, all those years ago is now long retired. A mutual friend of ours was very sick, and he asked us to join him at a church service recently. Imagine that, going to church with your former co-workers? I was totally okay with this, but I knew that not everyone would be. When I asked my former boss if he would like to join us, not surprisingly, he said no. Thinking supply chain management here (sometimes you have more power in indirect places), I invited his wife instead; I knew that she had a beautiful heart and would want to be there for our former colleague. Mission accomplished! As predicted, she and her husband (my former boss) were both in attendance.

I wound up buying lunch for everyone after the service, and my old boss emailed later and said, "Wow, Michaela—that was really nice, and if you ever do anything like that again for him, then I will be happy to pay for lunch." He went on to praise the day and comment on how great it was to be around our former crew and how much it obviously meant for our sick colleague. You see, he really did have a heart in there, and it had been touched that day.

This was a bit of a personal victory, because I knew that this man would most likely come and visit me in the hospital if, in fact, I was dying from cancer. But his point was well taken. Don't waste your time trying to make other people happy; you can only be responsible for your own happiness.

YOUR PERSONAL BOARD OF DIRECTORS

I was fortunate to meet Jack Welch (General Electric's former chairman and CEO) in a hotel lobby in San Francisco back in the early 90s. I wasn't fully aware of how influential Jack Welch and General Electric were at the time, but he introduced me to a concept that evening that caught my attention. Think of your life like a company. You're the president and CEO (ME, Inc.). Now who do you want around you as your C-level executives? Who would you invite to be on ME, Inc.'s board of directors? The people who you choose to have around you, particularly in an advisory role, have the potential to make or break the whole operation, so give it some serious thought.

For the sake of an example, I'll share with you how MICHAELA,

Inc. is currently structured. My personal board of directors includes an accountant (because I couldn't care less about money, he's my Chief Financial Officer; ironically, I have to pay him to be on my board), my wingman (every girl needs one of these), a psychic (because her talent mystifies my scientific brain, she's my Chief Psychic Officer), a minister (because I have recently started exploring spirituality, she's my Chief Spiritual Officer), a dressage riding instructor (she's my Chief Riding Officer), a marksman (he's my Chief Handgun Officer), a race car driver (he's my Chief Driving Instructor), and a handful of others.

Now some of these people are professionals who I have to pay for their support, but others are people who I simply find inspirational and who I approached out of the blue. It's as simple as reaching out to people and asking them to be on your personal board of directors. Their first question is normally, "What in the heck is a personal board of directors?" I then explain that I consider them to be exceptional in a particular area that I would like to personally grow in, and I am hoping that they would be willing to take me under their wings and teach me. Their next question is normally, "What do I have to do?" I then explain that I would simply like to take them out to lunch or dinner a few times a year and listen to their advice and teaching along the lines of their respective specialty area. To which they normally reply, "Sure!"

People almost never say no when asked to participate on someone's personal board of directors. Why? Because people genuinely like helping other people; it's human nature. They are also quite flattered that you consider them to be an expert in something. You would be surprised at how high of a level you can go with your requests. It doesn't involve a huge time commitment on their end, and the benefits to both of you are immeasurable. Try it, and you will see.

Think about the power of having five to seven people, whose advice and counsel you value, and meeting them quarterly to discuss *you*, and *you* alone. They're like angels, with wings that are stronger than yours, pulling you up higher than your present state. And all they are really doing in that meeting is teaching you how to be a better you. They are all joined in a singular focus as well, i.e., caring about you. I don't dare call this "love," but on some level, that is what we are talking about here. You'll find out quickly that this feels pretty good, and it does wonders for your knowledge base, confidence, mind, body, heart, and soul.

This same approach can be used indirectly to help other people who are struggling emotionally. My daughter, Nikki, was being bullied when she was in high school and, as a result, was getting depressed, but I (or even worse, a psychiatrist) was the last person on the planet who she would agree to talk to about any of this.

So, I thought to myself, Nikki needs a personal board of directors comprised of people whom she trusts. Thus, I set about speaking to the people in her life who were the most influential, i.e., one of her teachers, her high school principal, her doctor, her nurse, her massage therapist (Nikki was struggling with her own medical issues at the time), and most importantly, her hair stylist (just think about how much regular face time Nikki spent with her hair stylist. Plus, this girl was hip!). All that I asked these individuals to do was to ask Nikki how she was feeling when they spent time with her; it was that simple! Ironically, after I explained what Nikki was coping with at school, they all enthusiastically agreed, except for one person—her older, male doctor at the Children's Hospital; no surprise there, but his nurse happily agreed.

The results were amazing; Nikki was significantly improved after only a few weeks of this personal board of directors' intervention. And when you think about this, all that I really asked these people to do was to help teach Nikki how to talk about her feelings. Each of them created a safe place for Nikki to share. What they did was essentially help guide Nikki to a healthier and happier place with their genuine love for her. With that much love and support in Nikki's life, it was next to impossible for her to continue to choose despair for herself.

There's a reason that you pick certain people to be on your board! You're at X point in your life, and they are at X plus a pretty significant delta higher than you are. The best part about this is that they are happy to pull you up. They are teaching, and teaching feels good too! The hidden, additional benefit with this exercise, and it took me a few years to figure this out, is that the more you associate with your supportive personal board of directors, the less time you have to spend with the negative people who drag you down. It's an opportunity cost of your time on this planet. Slowly, you'll teach yourself how to sort out the good and healthy role models in your life, and it's as simple as asking them for help. We can't do certain things all by ourselves, and no one is perfect. So, admit your imperfections, assemble your personal board of directors, and take control of your own life, just as if *you* were a real corporation!

For the life of me, I cannot figure out why more people do not do this. Why is no one investing in themselves? This Jack Welch-inspired board of directors idea is completely free and incredibly empowering. It's choosing to surround yourself with positive, intelligent, loving, giving, and uplifting people. Even the Millennials (who, if you ask them, think that they know everything) don't know about this. I find that guys, in particular, are especially resistant to trying this idea. They think it's kind of dorky at first, but once they understand and realize its powerful benefits, they quickly jump on board. :)

WRITING YOUR OWN JOB DESCRIPTION

Okay, now that you have assembled your own personal board of directors, it's time to sort out what you are actually going to do at work. People complain all the time about not having a job description. I hear this more times than I can count, and I have to say that it drives me a little crazy, especially because people blame their manager or their boss or their corporation for not having one in place. If the lack of a job description is truly preventing you from understanding what you are supposed to be doing at work, then by all means, go write your own! What's stopping you?

I was working with a team of executives a number of years

ago, all of whom were at the vice president level or above, and they were all whining and complaining about not having job descriptions. This situation had been going on for well over a year. Are you kidding me? It was fairly shocking honestly. I added up how many years of directly applicable experience this team of individuals had, and it was close to two hundred combined years. Baby boomers have a tendency to be pretty passive-aggressive and suffer in silence over life's little insults, but when they get together in a group, they start to feed off of each other and compare injustices. This particular group was really going to town.

I told every one of them to stop waiting for someone else to do this, and instead, volunteer to write their very own job descriptions. This is a classic example of a group of people who don't understand that no one else is going to care about them if they don't care about themselves first. There's a reason that they don't have job descriptions that match what they do. If they don't care about themselves and their careers enough to take the bull by the horns and create what they need to succeed, then why on this green earth should anyone else?

There are a wealth of resources and tools online to help you craft your own job description. The Millennials have tapped into this already, because remember, they are instinctually programmed to go find what they need and make it happen. I've seen Millennials take no more than two hours to thoroughly research and write their job descriptions and then go marching into their boss's office and announce that they should be paid more. Salary.com and salaryfinder.com are web-based resources that allow you to see where you fall in the salary category according to your level, your location, your experience, etc. Any website that posts jobs will have job descriptions posted as well. The information is out there, so go use it to your advantage.

JOB FAMILY PLANNING

If your boss hasn't already drawn you a very clear map of the reporting structure within your company, along with the associated job families that exist to support this structure, then you will need to do this yourself as well. How else are you going to be able to plan for the next three to five years? You need to know where you're going in order to get there!

Understanding the hierarchy of your organization, and the way various positions align in your position's "job family," is an important step in creating a job description that will provide you a realistic framework with which to move forward. I tend to work primarily in laboratory settings, thus a typical job family would consist of the following: an introductory lab assistant 1 (zero to one years of experience) and a lab assistant 11 (three to fiveyears of experience), but there is also a senior lab assistant (more than five years of experience), a supervisor, a manager, a director, a senior director, and a vice president. See how that works?

You need to understand how many years and what kind of experience you will need to advance to the next level. This is true of any profession or industry. You cannot rely on others to map your career path for you. Start by identifying where you are today. Don't be afraid to approach your boss and say, "Hey, Joe. Can you please help me understand what the job family that I am in looks like?" Hopefully Joe has an answer for you, but don't be surprised if he doesn't. If your boss is clueless and doesn't have this information immediately accessible, then go find the information you need yourself. It's out there. HR may also be able to help you.

Next, consider asking Joe if the two of you can work together to map out a plan for your continued advancement there. If your boss cannot show you the job description that follows the position that you are currently in, then not only do you not have a proper career path intentioned for yourself, but you probably don't have a very good boss either.

Lay out your own plan to get to the next level in your organization and identify what you will need to get there. Do you need an advanced degree or additional qualifications? How many people will you be expected to manage? What kind of courses do you need to take? What are the performance expectations for each of the roles in the job family? This is all just a part of taking an active interest in yourself and putting in the legwork to get ahead. If the prospect of crafting a career development plan is overwhelming, consult with your personal board of directors or add someone to it who can coach you forward.

If things are not going the way you want them to go, ask for help. Do something! Blaming your boss will get you nowhere. Playing the victim and complaining about your lot in life is no way to get ahead. So many times, more times that I care to even think about, when I tell people to go write their own job descriptions, the response is "Oh my gosh. I can't do that! That's my boss's job." To which I respond, "If you ever want to be the boss, then start helping your own boss by demonstrating some initiative!"

Baby boomers and others who are stuck in the Command-and-Control mentality have a particularly hard time accepting responsibility for themselves. It's a whole new way of thinking, and people in general are oftentimes resistant to change. But think about it. If you want to be heard, and more importantly, accurately measured and evaluated, doesn't it make sense to take it upon yourself to create (and know) the metrics? If you are working with a job description that is three years or older and you have a performance evaluation coming up, rewrite that thing! Your boss will be impressed that you took the time and the initiative to create a realistic barometer for yourself. He will also be happy that you've done his work for him.

ENROLLING OTHERS IN YOUR OWN SUCCESS

When I refer to enrolling others in your own individual success, I am essentially talking about adopting a tribe mentality. There is a fine line between taking responsibility for yourself and doing it *all by yourself.* We all need support, encouragement, and feedback to thrive. No man is an island, and the sooner you recognize the importance of the people around you, and how they contribute to or detract from your own success, the better off you'll be. You don't want to alienate your co-workers by marching around promoting yourself, but you don't want to rely solely on the voice of the team to be heard either.

Here's an example of what happens when you try to forge on ahead alone and ignore the tribe. I was working with a company recently that needed to put together a brand new organization, complete with Quality and Regulatory (Q&R) resources. One of the Directors of Q&R had been working on a strategy for the new organization, and she had the whole thing pretty much figured out. She assembled the strategy on her own, forged ahead, and presented her plan to the organization's team quite eloquently.

Guess what happened? She bombed. Miserably. This poor girl was practically booed out of the boardroom. She delivered a beautiful presentation to a leadership team of C-level players, and they shut her down completely. Ouch.

Now, what did she do wrong? She didn't enroll anyone else in her success! It doesn't matter that her presentation was well thought-out and dead on from a Q&R perspective. She neglected to engage the participants in her solution, and for that primary reason, she was shut down. The tribe had spoken.

Later, she asked me what she had done wrong, and I explained the importance of enrolling others in her own success. She was in a tough spot because she was visiting from another country and didn't know anyone on the team. Plus, it was a brand new organization. She didn't have a clue about who she should have talked to and why it even mattered. She was the Q&R specialist, and she had presented a Q&R plan. How and why did this go so terribly wrong?

I asked her who she thought had the most institutional power in the organization. (Hint: It's normally not the person highest on the organization chart.) I told her that she blew it because she didn't ask anyone for input, feedback, or support. In this particular organization, the person with the most institutional power was Mary, the administrative assistant to the CEO. Mary had been there from the very beginning, she knew everyone, and she knew who would have been able to help her get connected.

I explained how much better her plan would have been received if only she had enlisted Mary's help in the beginning. If she had said, "Mary, listen. I want to make an impact with my plan. I don't know anyone here. Who do you think I should talk to? Who are the best people to work with, and what are their strengths? Can I ask you to help me track this for the next few months?" She would have made a friend for life, who in turn would have put her in touch with the right people. Do you see how this works? Plus, Mary would have been flattered for being recognized as a power player as well.

Interestingly, administrative assistants in Europe oftentimes title their email signatures and business cards with "Sr. Executive Administrative Assistant to Dr. X"; Dr. X's status in the corporation is frequently directly correlated to that of their administrative assistant's as well. Leave it to the Europeans to put it out there like that; these administrative assistants are essentially saying, "I have this much power in this organization because this is who I support here!" Pay attention to the supply chain of power at work, folks. Sometimes an indirect path will get you the highest return on your individual investment.

Please note that I was not trying to "woulda, coulda, shoulda" her out of her fix, but instead, I illustrate the importance of asking for help. Asking for help doesn't mean that you're weak. It means that you're looking out for yourself. And remember, if you don't do it, nobody else will. It's quite literally chapter one all over again.

CHAPTER 2

FINDING YOUR HEART

THE GOAL OF EVERY MANAGER SHOULD BE TO ALIGN
what the company needs as a corporation with what his/her
employee's hearts have to give. That's not always the way a
manager approaches the relationship, but for true mutual
success to occur, that is how it *needs* to be.

The company's initiatives are only half of this equation.
The company's goals start at the top and need to be clearly
communicated down to the staff so that they can determine
if they are on board and aligned. It's everyone's individual
responsibility to dig deep and look at their own goals and
determine if there is overlap. Think about it. When we go
to work, we are not on an extended play date. We are there
to service the needs of the organization and to finance our
personal lives. It's pretty hard to be in touch with what an
employee can offer the company if the manager is not in
touch with who their employee is as a person, what drives

them, and where their true personal passions lie. If the employee's goals don't align with the company's, then it's simply not a good fit.

PERMISSION TO LOOK FOR IT

Now, here's where things can get a little tricky. How many people, employees, or managers are truly in touch with their hearts? Or to make this sound a little more professionally rational, how many people ever articulate their list of personal, intrinsic drivers to their boss (e.g., an amazing title, work/life balance, a high salary, a difficult problem to solve, a short commute)? Sadly, almost nobody does. This is a discovery and a truth that can only come from within. As a manager and someone who knows that people are never going to thrive until they have found their hearts, I always try to encourage my staff to get in touch with the driving force, or forces, within them. But I cannot do this for them. I wish I could, but it absolutely has to come from inside of them.

I can ask a string of questions that prompt people to think about their lives in a new way. What I've discovered, and as you might imagine, this is where things get personal very quickly.

At the end of the day, we are all animals, which is really important to remember. (It's amazing to me how often my undergraduate degree in Animal Science helps out at work.) Not only are we all animals, but we are herd animals, which means that we desire closeness and a sense of community; isolation equals death. So what I do, as has been mentioned previously, is take my own ego out of my body and put it on the shelf in that moment, and I genuinely show up for the person and actively listen to them. As corny as that may sound, it's true. That's my secret, and that's how I've helped many people find their hearts at work. It's as simple as giving them permission to do so, because if they don't know what's in their heart, there's no way that I can figure this out for them; I'm not that psychic—yet. :)

Together, we are stripping away their armor that says, "Don't surrender, and whatever you do, don't tell her!" But once the armor is off and you can see where your heart is guiding you and you can communicate what it's saying, then you can start to look at yourself in a new way. I sometimes ask, "What are you running from? What are you afraid of? Why are you looking at the ground instead of the sky?" When you look at the ground, your heart is closed, and if you start looking at the sky, it will help open your heart. Pay attention to this the next time you're outside. Where is your heart guiding you? It's okay. Just start paying attention to the things that motivate you professionally.

Once you stop running and give yourself permission to look up instead of down, and to look in instead of out, you'll start to find it. It might be a little bit scary, but there's nothing to be afraid of. It's the most beautiful thing that you'll ever discover on this planet. It's also the one thing in life that will never betray you.

Your heart is one of the very few things that will be with you forever. Your money, your titles, your degrees, your bosses, your peers, your performance ratings are not going to matter as you are taking your last breath. Your heart is at the core of what you bring to the table for your corporation. And more importantly, this is who you are as an individual.

Until you get in touch with your heart, your manager cannot pair you up with the duties that are required at work, because—if you think about it—you want to be happy, and your manager wants to be happy. This is basically a matching game, i.e., aligning what the company needs to get done with what you want to do.

YOUR PERSONAL INTRINSIC DRIVERS

Your heart's signals come from all directions. When confused with regards to this whole idea, sometimes simply looking at your heart "based on results" as to where your heart has already taken you, or is currently taking you, is helpful. Rational thinkers like these exercises the best. For example:

1. What classes have you taken? What degrees do you have?

2. What jobs have you liked? What jobs have you not liked? And why?

3. What do you like to do for fun?

4. Rank ten things in your life in order of importance to you.

5. Keep a daily journal and then look at what your heart is already choosing.

Finding your heart can be a tactical process. You need to take a personal assessment of your own intrinsic drivers and think about what motivates you: is it money, a big title, managing others, family, time off, a shorter commute, or work/life balance? List your motivators in order of importance. This assessment helps you to identify the why (you are the way you are) and the how (you can live in harmony with your heart). What do you bring to the table that no one else does? And as soon as you have this critical piece sorted out, attach it to your mouth, and then share it with your boss!

I know it's hard. Finding your heart is not easy. I'm not going to dive too much into the how-to on this topic, because it's a different route in for everyone. But if I were to take a poll of all the people who I have worked with over the years, they will tell you that my insistence on them finding their heart professionally was the hardest thing that I ever asked them to do. I can't give people the formula, but I can help them think it through analytically.

THE SPROUT PROGRAM

I was hired not too long ago by a company to oversee a turnaround. I was told that there wasn't going to be any quality unless I ran Operations as well. When I'm brought in, I expect a mess. That's why I get asked, or hired, to fix it. But this laboratory in particular needed an overhaul from top to bottom, and we were going to have to hire at all levels: lab assistants, clinical laboratory scientists, managers, everyone.

Once I started the interview process with external and

internal people, I realized that there wasn't anyone there who could actually *lead* anything. As a result, I came up with the SPROUT program. Leaders aren't made in this space, so we were going to have to grow, or "sprout," them ourselves. Get it? Cute, huh? :)

SPROUT is an acronym (isn't everything these days?) for "sprouting" new leaders. The "SP" stands for special projects. Right off the bat (and first in the word because it is the most important) finding your heart came into play with Special Projects. Unless people were in touch with their hearts, they could not participate in or lead a Special Project. Why? Because Special Projects require that the people working on them are truly devoted and passionate about that particular project. I couldn't assign these to people. They needed to tell me which project they were drawn to, and to do so, they needed to be in touch with their hearts. I basically said, "This process requires deep self-exploration. Go meditate, fly a kite, call your therapist. I don't know. Just go do it. It's one of the most important pieces of knowledge that you will ever discover in your life. If you don't find and then follow your heart, you'll never be happy." This at least got them all thinking about doing things very differently.

This group of scientists was preparing for a very high-end, high tech Silicon Valley molecular test that no one else on the planet knew how to run. Everyone there was completely titillated by it. I wanted them to understand that although the test was extremely high profile and potentially career shaping, the *most* important thing, at the end of the day, was to find their hearts and then find a way to bring that uniqueness into the workplace. That uniqueness, and ultimately work-place satisfaction, leads to happiness on the deepest level, which is something that I think everyone strives for, whether they are willing to admit it or not. This is why the "SP" in SPROUT comes first.

The "ROU" in SPROUT stood for routine operations. I wanted the staff to learn that receiving reagents, taking out the trash, and sweeping the floor are just as important as performing the fancy laboratory test itself. I wanted them to develop a healthy appreciation for everyday systems and the things that they may have taken for granted until now. Also, the "ROU" accounted for the majority, core of the program, and their work.

The "T" in SPROUT stood for "testing"—or actually performing the fancy molecular test that they all wanted so eagerly to learn immediately after being hired; yet strategically, I had placed it at the end of the word on purpose, because over the course of their careers, the various tests that they would learn were going to come and go; their heart, however, was going to serve them for their entire lifetime.

A TEACHING HEART

Jacqueline was a participant in the SPROUT program, and she knew what I was going for. She was really young, in her mid-20s, and she came to me early on and told me that she was afraid of the "finding your heart thing." Now, I give her a lot of credit because just saying that out loud was a brave statement, and it started the conversation. We talked about what she was afraid of and why and what that fear looked like. She was pretty lost, no doubt, and skeptical, but she was eager to figure it out. Willingness does wonders for the heart!

She told me that she had an aunt who had invited her to Sedona over the summer. She was really nervous about going because her aunt was into meditation and spirituality, and it scared the pants off of Jacqueline. She had no idea what she was getting herself into. I encouraged her to just go, because I strongly believe that when the student is ready, the teacher appears, and Jacqueline was clearly ready.

I have no idea what happened out there in Sedona with Jacqueline and her aunt, but she came back reborn. She had figured it out. She wanted to be a teacher. She figured out that she loved to read, go to school, and give. The interesting thing about Jacqueline's Sedona experience is that she went into it thinking that she might want to be a park ranger, but after spending all of that time outdoors, she learned for sure that she definitely did not want to be a park ranger ever. Sometimes learning what your heart doesn't care about can be equally as valuable as what your heart does care about. Jacqueline had come back from Arizona able to communicate that her personal, intrinsic drivers centered on teaching others.

Ironically, and here's where the matching piece comes to the table, the company was badly in need of a Training Coordinator at the time. Jacqueline had just graduated from her graduate training program, and she knew that Training Coordinator positions are typically reserved for people with significant work experience. And for this reason, Jacqueline had not inquired about the opportunity. Had Jacqueline's heart been attached to her mouth in the first place, she could have intentioned this job for herself much sooner. Instead, I helped facilitate the matching for her. To this day, Miss Jacqueline is one of the happiest and best Training Coordinators that I have ever met.

THE CLOSED HEART

I've been through the heart finding process with hundreds of people at this stage in my career. Everyone's journey is unique, and each story blows my mind in its own special way.

Suzette was hands down one of the most closed people I had ever met when we first crossed paths many years ago. She came to interview with me, and right away, she told me the top five reasons why I should *not* hire her. Who says that? Did she really want the job or not? I was confused, but I had a hunch about her. I have a pretty strong intuition, and I can read people, especially givers. Something told me that I should look a little deeper into this candidate, even though she had bombed the interview.

I called her advisor from graduate school and said, "Doctor, I want to talk to you about Suzette." His response? "She's the best student that we have ever had in this program." I said, "She's the worst person that I've ever interviewed, but my heart tells me that she's probably the best person I could ever hire." He said, "Michaela, listen to your heart." We both agreed that she might not survive the interview with HR. He said, "Do what you need to do to get her around any other interviews, but I'm telling you that she'll be the best hire you've ever...no, she'll be the best human being you've ever hired in your life." Well, that's a pretty strong testimonial, and my emotional intelligence was in complete agreement. So, I helped to get her hired.

Things didn't go so swimmingly with Suzette straight away. When she first came to work, she announced, "I do not like animals" and "I don't ever want to lead people." I didn't know where these feelings were coming from, but I did know that she didn't have any pets and she had never led anyone in her life. Clearly, Suzette was going to be a challenge. Her heart was closed up like a vault.

Over time, we chipped away at her defenses together. We were in a lab setting, and everyone had pets, which is not uncommon. Most of the people in this environment were animal lovers. I started very small and very safely with Suzette. Little by little, and this took about three to four years, she ever so slowly started to open up. One day, she came into work and announced that she had adopted a cat! Not a full-grown cat either but a lovable, cuddly, teensy, tiny, adorable kitten. We all just about fell off of our respective lab stools. VICTORY!!!!

But it didn't stop there. Once she opened her heart a crack and experienced love, she got another cat. To this day, these cats have been the absolute center of her universe. From the cats, she moved on to leading people, just one employee at first and then a few more. She loves her employees as much as she loves her cats.

Two jobs ago, I left the department in her hands. She's an amazing leader, and she has more love and joy in her life than she ever imagined possible. Suzette clearly had a lot of hidden talents; they were simply hidden behind a closed heart, and in a safe and accepting environment, she was able to bring them to bear.

We joke about her clamped up heart now. To this day, Suzette will tell you, "Michaela knows me better than I know myself." And she,s even graduated to "Michaela understands me better than I will let myself understand myself." My how the doctor was right.

A WOUNDED HEART

Of course, there are sadly a good number of people who are so closed and broken that they don't belong in the workplace at all. It's not hard to spot these people, but it can be a challenge to help them understand that they need a break. This comes back to my secret of genuinely caring about people and giving them a safe space; sometimes this means giving them a safe space to completely fall apart.

There was a woman I worked with once who became very emotional during our one-on-one conversations. It was clear that there was something going on in her life that was way bigger than her job. Many of my questions led to teary responses, and I was concerned enough to come out and ask her to help me understand where the tears were coming from.

She confided in me that she had lost a child, her very young daughter, a couple of years earlier. She had devoted 100% of her life to caring for the child, and being in a medical environment was a painful reminder to her of what she had lost. Over the course of our discussions, it became clear that her heart was shattered in pieces. She needed to heal herself; she was literally emotionally incapable of working. The only thing that I could give her at the time was the permission to let herself resign and a book called *Unattended Sorrow*, which is about unresolved grief (although I think that it's more about loving than it is about grieving). It didn't happen overnight, but eventually she went on to bigger and better things. Most importantly, she removed herself from a workplace situation that was causing her to suffer immensely.

Sometimes people need a shrink instead of a job. Think about this. There are situations such as this woman's that occur in the workplace every day; they are clearly outside of a boss's ability to manage or control. Unfortunately, there are many severely depressed employees in the workforce. These people need help. They should not be working for anyone else; these people need to be taking care of themselves instead.

A LITTLE PATIENCE

If you're lost, own it. Breathe in to the fact that you're lost, or put it on the shelf for another day.

I'll tell you a story about my employee Cathy. When she first came to me, she was in the middle of a horrific divorce. She had two small children and was living in temporary housing. She was seriously lost, and she knew it; at the time, she was simply happy to just have a job. The last thing that she needed (or maybe the *first* thing she needed) was her boss saying to her, "Welcome to work today, Cathy! Guess what? We're going to help you find your heart here!"

Cathy was frustrated because her colleagues all around her had already found their hearts; they were rocking and rolling, and she felt a little left out. I encouraged her to keep listening to her heart when faced with a new initiative. She'd try a project for six or eight months, but she just knew that she wasn't feeling it. Her head was at least aiming in the "search" direction, and this meant that it was open.

It was very difficult for Cathy, but she kept at it, slow and steady, trying and listening and waiting. About a year and a half in, she found it! What she found was a big surprise to everyone. She had been edging towards a leadership role for a while, but when she found her heart, she realized that she wanted to perform research as an individual contributor instead. Not surprisingly, this was in complete alignment with the PhD degree that she had earned years earlier. Once she unearthed her calling, there was no turning back. I was so proud of her! All of that work ultimately led her to a transformative moment in her professional life. And there's another very important lesson here; it's perfectly fine if you do not want to ever lead other people!

I can't force people to go in if they are not willing or ready. They just need to be clear with me about their intentions.

If they want to leave the heart piece alone, we can look at what their brains and feet are telling them instead; this is a lot safer place to start. The sad thing about all of this is that most people on this planet (especially women) go to their graves without ever truly discovering their hearts. But I can tell you that very few of my employees ever will!

ATTACHING YOUR HEART TO YOUR MOUTH

Once you find your heart, you will then need to be able to speak for it. There are two distinct and critical steps that comprise the crux of your inevitable success. First, you need to find your heart, and then you need to attach it to your mouth (think Katy Perry's, "Roar" song here) for me, your boss, to play corporate matchmaker with it.

If I notice an introverted employee trying to crawl into his lab coat unnoticed, I'll speak to that person privately. I explain to them that sadly the business world values extroversion significantly more than it values introversion, thus extroversion, whether we like it or not, is rewarded in the workplace. The sooner you attach your mouth to your heart, the sooner you're actually going to start letting everybody else know how you feel as well. Don't forget that everyone must bring their own heart to the workplace table, and speaking up is a big part of how to champion for yourself.

I had one particularly quiet employee who rarely spoke. He was a very good worker, and everyone really enjoyed working with him. But he was so quiet that he was rarely noticed by upper management.

He and I worked hard on helping him attach his heart to his mouth. We started out very slowly and safely (imagine that) by me simply asking him to try mentioning at least one thing out loud during our weekly staff meetings. I told him that it didn't matter what he talked about—it could be anything. I knew that he was totally into UFC fighting (there's no talking required in the Octagon either :)), and so was I. I asked him to simply give us a UFC fight update each week. This was actually kind of funny because not very many of the other team members were into UFC fighting, but before long, as you can imagine, everyone looked forward to his weekly fight night updates!

The next step was to try to mainstream his messaging a little. At the time, everyone in our department was obsessed with a podcast from National Public Radio (NPR) called "Serial." I suggested that he switch from UFC updates to Serial recaps for those who weren't able to listen to it. Little by little, inch by inch, we started making it safer for him to speak up, and now, he roars a fair bit more.

In a typical corporate environment, if he was lucky, they would have sent someone like him to a pricey public speaking forum for a couple of weeks and told him to get over it. At most companies, he would have simply been ignored. In some cases, he would have been fired for not collaborating or contributing to the team. I see at it as my job, and my responsibility, to give people the tools and the encouragement, and above all, a safe place to soar.

Think for a minute about the name or title that you ask

people to call you. Is it even your real name? Do you really want your co-workers to call you this? How do you feel when you are called your name or your title at work?

For well over a year, we called one of our lab assistants "Susan" because that is what she told us her real name was; her real name was not Susan—it was a beautiful, ethnic name instead. Over the course of her safe, personal journey with us, she found her heart, attached it to her mouth, and developed the courage to tell all of us that her real name was not "Susan." Ironically, this all happened just about the same time that we were hiring a legit "Susan"—and as a result of her telling us what her name really was, we never had to deal with keeping two different Susans straight. :)

My management style differs significantly from others in that I recognize the inherent value of individuals' hearts, not only to the bodies that they are in but also to the greater organization as a whole. I create a safe environment where talking about employee's intrinsic professional drivers is the accepted norm. People trust me because they can sense that I really care about them. And I want to teach them that it's okay to care about themselves and each other too.

I've had a number of employees ask me to take it a step further, because they want to move beyond just attaching their mouths to their hearts at work. And for this, I outsource them, because come on, let's be honest. I'm their boss, not their spiritual advisor!

I've referred a few employees to a book titled *The Untethered*

Soul: The Journey Beyond Yourself by Michael A. Singer. The interesting thing about this book is that I bought it at a bookstore only because it had a horse on the cover (I love horses!), and I thought that it was written by a girl named Michaela, but after looking closer, I realized that it was written by Michael A. instead. The universe never ceases to amaze me. It's a very enlightening book for it takes you beyond your heart and more. Check it out when you're ready.

CHAPTER 3

WHO'S THE BOSS?

CHOOSING WHO TO WORK FOR IS ONE OF THE MOST important decisions that people make, and nine times out of ten, they make it blindly. Your boss has the highest return on investment with regard to your career than any other person within the organization. He or she is going to have access to information and processes that will impact you significantly. Deciding who to work for is a lot like dating if you think about it. You are entering into a relationship with this person, and they will directly impact your daily reality.

INTERVIEWING BACK

People rarely consider the importance of their future boss until it's too late. When you're interviewing for a new job, the strong tendency is to focus solely on getting in the door. Red flags and gut instincts are overridden by the desire to land the position. You think, "Hey, this guy seems like a real jerk. But I'll worry about that later. Most people hate their boss anyway, right? Once he sees how great my work is, he'll calm down, right?" Wrong! Once a jerk, typically always a jerk. People rarely change.

I interview people all the time. Making the right hire is a huge part of my job, and my screening process is very detailed, as you might imagine. Very rarely have I ever been asked any hard questions back from a candidate during an interview. It's perfectly acceptable, when interviewing for a job, to interview back. I really don't understand why more people don't do this. Go ahead and ask the questions that will put them on the spot and reveal their true management style. It's your professional life that you're about to put in their bossy hands.

There are certain questions that can get right to the heart of who that person is as an individual. Don't be afraid to go there. This is *your* life and *your* time! Make them squirm a little bit. You should go in with eyes wide open. Consider asking the following:

- How would one of your employees (or your boss) describe you?
- What do you like (or not like) about working here?
- Have you ever fired anyone?
- When was the last time you put someone on a performance improvement plan?
- How do you lead? Can you describe your leadership style?
- If you had a day off and $500 in cash, how would you spend it?
- What are the attrition rates for your department? (Don't

be surprised when they tell you that they don't measure this.)
- Why would anyone want to join, or leave, your organization? Or this company?
- What is your relationship like with HR?
- What do you do for fun?
- Have you ever been in an argument with anyone at work?
- Are you happy working here?
- How much "juice" do you have at this company?

These are all perfectly legal questions, and you can tell right away when someone is lying. And besides, rational, business-minded people search for these kinds of metrics. It can all be gauged very succinctly. For you rational readers, go ahead and ask the questions that are measurable!

MY AFRICAN TRUST FALL

Trust is the cornerstone of every relationship, and the one you have with your boss, or the person that you hire, is no different. I learned about the slippery trust slope when I went on a science safari in Tanzania, Africa a number of years ago. I did an exchange program with a professor from the University of Dar es Salaam and taught microbiology there for six weeks.

As a white, American female on my own at times, I was advised to hire a personal guide to essentially protect me. It's volatile over there, and crime was rampant in some parts of the cities that we were in. We had multiple field trips planned and camping overnight in the Serengeti to collect molecular samples. The danger of being kidnapped just driving through town was high.

I trusted the person who I was exchanging with to select the right guide for me. When I got over there, sure enough, my guide greeted me at the airport with his guns, and I thought to myself, "Cool. This is going to be fun!"

It occurred to me, more than once, to ask myself who's the real boss here? I was paying this guy, I felt like I had all the power and all the control in the relationship, but did I really? I know that I did not interview him or question him in any way before arriving. I just showed up in Africa, he had some guns, and away we went. A lot of crazy things happened over there (too many to go into detail here). There was a lot of corruption underway, and an American woman like me could fetch a pretty high price from kidnappers on the black market.

The exchange wound up lasting about two and half months, and during that time, the guide and I had been through some pretty harrowing experiences together. At the end of the trip, I gave him a $5,000 tip, which was pretty significant in those days (and still is!). He just looked at me and said, "I'm not sure that this is enough money, Michaela." Well, I was absolutely dumbfounded and very confused. Maybe this really wasn't enough money. I was worried that I had possibly insulted him.

He explained, "Michaela, you are way too trusting. I don't think you really understood who the real boss on this trip was." He told me that he was approached several times by kidnappers and even cited a few occasions in which I had been present right there on the scene—i.e., occasions where I had no idea what was going on, and he was doing all the talking and negotiating. Sometimes I was asked to hand over money (which at the time I had thought was for bribes to enter the area). I was horrified at how close I had actually been to very real danger without even knowing it, all while my life had been in the hands of a complete stranger. I had trusted him blindly, and he gave me absolutely no reason to do so.

My guide could have easily, and on several occasions, made ten times what I had offered him as a tip by selling me to the kidnappers. He could have been a king by Tanzanian standards with that kind of money, so I asked him, "Why didn't you sell me to them then?" He laughed out loud, for we had gotten to know each other pretty well during this short period of time. He said, "I'm going to tell you the truth, Michaela. I seriously did consider selling you in the beginning. But you have taught me many things, and after some time, I grew to kind of like you. Plus, I know that you are really smart (apparently the kidnappers aren't very smart), and I thought that you just might escape from them and then I know for sure that you would come hunt me down soon afterwards. So, now I give you this learning. You are too trusting. You need to think about who the real boss here was." Turns out, in that scenario, it wasn't me; my African guide was the boss the entire time. No doubt.

So, who are you blindly giving the power over you away to?

Leading others is an honor and a privilege; it's not a given right. Remember that, and think before you allow someone to lead you, trust them with your entire professional career, or most importantly, trust them with your life. I learned this the hard way in Africa. Thank goodness that money was not at the top of my guide's intrinsic, personal motivators list!

TOXIC BOSSES

"Toxic handling" is a term that is popping up in management circles these days. It's growing to be a very real science. Scientists are learning that some human beings are so toxic that they can actually hurt other people, both physically and emotionally. Then, there is another group of people dubbed "toxic handlers" who enable this toxic behavior by cleaning up after them, making excuses for them, or in some cases, actually rewarding them for their bad behaviors. Toxic handlers are similar to the codependents of alcoholics or drug addicts.

The Internet is chock full of resources to help you find out if you have or are enabling a toxic boss. Just Google the term, and you'll come up with a list of questions to ask yourself to get to the root of the issue. When people go online and see the many associated toxic boss surveys that exist, it really resonates.

They are then able to very clearly identify the character traits of all of the toxic people around them. Oftentimes, it's not just the boss; it can be a partner, spouse, sister, parent, or best friend. These people can be overcome and dealt with, but it's a matter of recognizing the characteristics and neutralizing them. It's also a matter of making the decision for yourself that you are not going to put up with this type of person or behavior in your life, and then taking the steps necessary to deal with it.

Knowledge is power. If you know going in what kind of person your boss is, then you can develop a strategy accordingly. Even if the boss is a complete jerk, you can take him or her on as a challenge, get and/or give what you are looking for with that company, and then get out of there. Sadly, you really do learn the most from the worst. Your toxic bosses inevitably make you stronger just in learning how to cope with them.

THE 50/50 RATIO

Keep in mind that every relationship is about balance. This is especially true of your relationship with your boss and your company. You both should be bringing equal parts to the table. It should be an even 50/50 split of energy and heart on both sides. If you bring 80% (of your possible 100% vote) and they bring 20% (of their possible 100% vote), well then, who do you think is going to feel mistreated and unappreciated? And what if you bring 100% and they bring 0%? Keep in mind that the most that you can ever vote is your own 100%, yet you are only responsible for half of the relationships. In both of these examples, the average of the combined votes is 50% (do the math!), and in most schools, that's an F, or one major epic FAIL of a relationship. In order for this relationship to work efficiently, and to the mutual benefit of both parties, it absolutely must be evenly balanced, with at least a combined score of something much closer to a passing grade!

I've been encouraging my employees to find their hearts and speak their truths, but this sentiment applies to leadership and upper management as well. Leaders are responsible for identifying the work that needs to be produced. I like to present my staff with an annual list of company initiatives. Employees need to know which of these initiatives they are going to support on their end. The company brings the goals, and the employees bring their personal intrinsic drivers with the intention of achieving them in a 50/50 balanced fashion. This is how the partnership between employees and leadership should function to be the most productive.

Most employees and leadership teams do not understand this crucial accountability component. The tendency is for unengaged employees to think, "I'm unhappy here. My boss sucks. It's his fault," and bosses tend to think, "Johnny's work sucks. I should probably think about getting rid of him some day" (and sadly, this is the norm).

BRASS RINGS

Do you remember those old wooden carousels with the horses and other animals? Back in the day, there were rings on little posts that stuck out, and as you rode past, you would try to grab as many of the rings as you could. Only one, or very few of them, were made of brass, and if you had the dexterity to grab the brass one, then you won a prize of some kind.

In my mind, as part of the 50/50 boss to employee relationship, it's my job to hand out all of the rings, including the brass ones, and for my employees, likewise, to grab a hold of them. If you don't want to stick your hand out and see what power the brass rings may have in store for you, that's okay, but it's still my job, as your boss, to make them available to you. I keep a few brass rings in my drawer at work, and I give them out on occasion; they are beautiful and meaningful to me, and they send this message home: When was the last time that anyone, including your boss, gave you the opportunity to grab a brass ring?

Really lame employees, who somehow make it through the interview process and turn out to have no desire for even a single brass ring, are still presented with the brass rings; this is what a good boss does. Most bosses don't even gather any rings in the first place, let alone hand them out to anyone else, and this is a huge problem. To get a brass ring, your boss needs to first offer it, and then you have to grab for it and pull; it requires *effort* on the part of both of you.

MANAGING BY WALKING AROUND (MBWA)

By now, you've likely noticed that I tend to focus on simple activities. Getting out of your office and walking around talking to people is a huge and very easy way to connect with your co-workers; sadly, most bosses rarely ever do it. You can't effectively own 50% of a relationship if you're just sitting in your office with the door closed all day long. Now, I know, almost no one is just sitting in their office, but seriously, leave the door open when you aren't on a private call, and better yet, take your legs out for a stretch. You'll be amazed at what you see and learn.

In the SPROUT program, the ROU stands for routine operations, remember? Walking around and looking to see if the garbage has been taken out or the black smudges have been removed from the floors is an opportunity to reconnect, even if it's over something mundane. You can't take the litmus test of an organization if you're not an active part of it. Go out and pay attention! Engage! It doesn't matter how high or how low you are on the totem pole. Walking around is a chance to gauge who holds the most institutional power, and don't forget to include the admins!

THE JUICE CARD

The primary difference between you and your boss is his or her degree of "juice," or power. The juice card is how much power one has in the workplace. Your boss is sort of like your parent at work from a power perspective; they have a lot more power than you do, and they are going to help you "grow up." Eventually, you hope to have a fuller juice card (and significantly more workplace power) as you move from good to great.

How many people do you know who think to ascertain the level of juice that their boss has during the interview process? With the hyperconnectivity of today's world, it should be fairly easy to find out what the boss's ratings are, e.g., by looking them up on websites like glassdoor.com. And if the online space is dark, simply ask the other employees. Ask the person who has the most institutional power, "What's it like to work for Joe? Does he take good care of his staff?" Whether you get a straight answer or not, that person's body language and reaction will speak volumes. Do yourself a favor and ask around before you accept the job offer.

When I first join a new company, I have little to no juice at all. The people who are technically below me on the totem pole have way more juice than I do. I admit it, and I'm okay with it for the time being. They are far more connected than I am in this new organization, and they are way more effective at getting things done in the beginning. We joke about it, but it's very true.

Eventually, I'll surpass them, but a huge part of stakeholder management is managing up, down, and all around. I consider it an honor for me to lead them and a privilege for me to learn from them. Because we talk and communicate all the time, I know that it makes them feel empowered, and it sure beats me walking in there and bossing everyone around, thereby spreading resentment and fear.

YOUR BOSS AND YOUR COMPANY

There are two critical components to your satisfaction at work, and they are mutually exclusive: the contribution of your boss and the culture of your company. You can work for the most amazing boss on the planet, but if you're both on the *Titanic* together, then you are both going down. The same goes for a luxury cruise through the Turks and Caicos; if you are there with a nightmarish, toxic boss, chances are that he'll sabotage your voyage. Neither situation will end happily. I know a fair number of people who worked for great bosses at startups that failed for financial reasons or who worked for horrible bosses at really good companies that are still in business today; both sets of individuals were equally miserable.

CHAPTER 4

PERFORMANCE MANAGEMENT

THE BOSS'S JOB IS TO MATCH THE COMPANY'S GOALS with the employees' hearts. I cannot emphasize this enough. In order for this 50/50 relationship to work, there needs to be communication. This involves setting clear expectations and goals.

FROM GOOD TO GOD

One of my main goals when I go into an organization is to help the employees make the move from good to great. I tell them this straight out of the gate so that everyone is clear on where they are going. I walk in assuming that everyone is already good, and if they are not good, they are likely going to exit the organization pretty quickly. Toxic employees tend go from bad to gone!

The highest return on a management's investment in an organization is simply carving out all of the bad (toxic) people. This activity is akin to removing the bad pieces from a delicious apple or the big boulders from an otherwise healthy and fast running stream. By removing these impediments, you are creating a safe workplace for nurturing the good ones to great.

I thrive on helping people discover their own potential and then living up to it. I feel like the catalyst in a chemical reaction, i.e., the reactions (their transformative change) occur faster and with less energy, and as the catalyst, I am not consumed. Instead, I am recycled (on to the next employee). Most people already think they are operating at a pretty high level, so when they achieve even more than they thought they could on their own, it can be quite mind blowing. They think, "What the heck just happened? How did she help get me to this new and amazing place?"

The key here is to create a safe environment for people to go bigger than they ever dreamed that they could. In essence, it's helping them connect with that greatness that's already within all of us. It comes from inside—it's the heart, the core, the delta, the essence (or whatever you want to call it) that takes you to another level altogether.

I was sharing this intention with a new, young manager when I first arrived at his company. Even though he was a novice at leading people, he was pretty cocky in most other areas. He had the hutzpah to announce, "Michaela, I think you're up for a challenge with me." And of course, my response was "Oh yeah? Why's that?" And he said, "Because I already think

I'm pretty great. So, good luck taking me from great to god, sister." Oh boy! Now this is the first person who has ever said anything even close to this to me after hundreds of employees. My response was "Well, at least you understand there's still room for improvement." And with that, the challenge was on. Managing high confidence employees is a whole new ball game, but my intention remains the same. While I have yet to take anyone from great to god, this guy is certainly going to try, and if he's game, then I am all in!

QUARTERLY MEETINGS

The boss needs to make him or herself available to the employee a minimum of four times a year to check in with the employee and evaluate their performance. Why quarterly? Well, the truth is that unless people know that they are going to meet with their boss again in ninety days, they just might go off the grid. Sad, but true! It's simply human nature.

These fixed meetings are devoted entirely to the growth and success of that particular individual employee. During this time, the employee's 50% contribution will be assessed according to metrics that the boss and the employee agreed on and put into place during the initial meeting. This is pretty basic stuff, but you'd be surprised at how many people completely overlook checking in with their boss or their employee, let alone doing so on a quarterly basis.

As an employee, if you care about yourself and your advancement, then it is in your own best interest to be proactive at scheduling these meetings and making sure that they happen. I do not schedule these meetings, and if they do not happen, then I consider this a loss to the employee. If they do not care enough about themselves to schedule these meetings, then why should I?

These meeting are just as important, if not more so, than writing your own job description. If you're not pushing yourself forward, then who else will do it? You cannot claim to be surprised if you are falling below expectations during your performance review if you never took the initiative to schedule these meetings. This is no more than a means of assuring your own success.

My strategy is to align the employee with the corporation's annual objectives. So, at the first meeting, I'll lead with my contributory 50% and identify the top goals of the company, and then I'll ask the employee to think about how he or she can personally contribute to them. It's pretty simple. I say, "Objective number one is to increase the company's profit by 5% quarter after quarter. Now, think about your own job and your own accountability. What do you think that looks like for you?" That's where I put the onus on them. This is letting them lead. I am purely acting as a catalyst.

The employee likely will not be able to contribute to *all* of the company's goals, and that's okay. More often what happens is the employee is able to attach their hearts to just one or two of the company goals, from which three to five personal goals emerge. The important part is that they are 100% clear on the company's plans for the year. As such, they can then meet the company in the middle and bring their 50% by fulfilling both their personal goals as well as the company's goals.

This is an extremely valuable undertaking in that it marries the employee's heart to the corporate bottom line. We all need to remember why we are here in the first place, which is to make money for the corporation and in turn make money for ourselves so that we can go home and finance our personal lives, remember? :)

And don't forget to conclude these quarterly meetings by providing feedback to your boss about his or her most recent performance as well. Your relationship with your boss is 50/50, and these meetings provide you with the perfect opportunity to let him or her know what you think about how well (or not) he or she has been performing.

SMART GOALS

Once the employees have a sense of how these quarterly meetings should go, they normally spend about 80% of the time doing the talking. The first session is an important one because together we establish what their personal goals are going to be for the coming year. Many people, believe it or not, have never even considered what their personal goals are, and if they have, they likely have not written them down anywhere or been held accountable for achieving them. Studies have proven that people are far more likely to achieve their goals if they actually write them down and review them on a regular basis.[3]

3   http://www.forbes.com/sites/85broads/2014/04/08/
    why-you-should-be-writing-down-your-goals

Goals may change or shift over the course of a year (this is perfectly fine by the way), which is another reason why it's important to meet on this topic regularly. The company goals may shift slightly too, and each employee would then need to modify their own accordingly.

Personal goals need to be SMART (oh, those acronyms in the workplace), which stands for specific, measurable, actionable, results-focused, and time-bound. There is an entire art and science around writing really good SMART goals, but as long as you capture each of the five elements, you are off to a good start.

One of my favorite goals pertains to simply exploring something new, and for this one, I oftentimes use the phrase "Explore the feasibility of bringing X vendor's technology into the workplace by Y date." While this particular goal did not commit to bringing the technology onboard, it afforded the leeway to explore such an idea. Using the "explore the feasibility of" verbiage can apply to a number of different scenarios. I suggest learning more about SMART goal writing online.

Scheduling the meetings falls to the employee. I constantly remind my employees that it is their job to be selfish with my time. My intention is to create behaviors and actions in which you take care of you. Your boss or direct manager is nowhere near as close to the successes or frustrations you have experienced since the first meeting ninety days ago. You need to come to the table prepared to share the good, the great, and the god! This is your opportunity to tout your accomplishments and identify areas where you need support.

Your boss or manager should come to the table prepared to say, "Help me understand how well you've done since the last time we met." In the (likely) event that your boss doesn't lead with a comment of that nature, by all means, take the reins and lead with "I'm excited to share with you how well things have been going since we last met," and then take it away! Sadly, most bosses only remember the things that you have screwed up over the course of the past ninety days. :(

Don't be surprised if you need to refocus your energies on a goal that didn't get as much attention in the last quarter. The purpose of these meetings is to promote *your* personal growth and *your* accomplishments. However, it is very important that your boss asks you what he or she can do to ensure that you are successful. This brings the accountability and support piece in on the boss's side.

In many situations, particularly in smaller organizations, the performance management system may not yet be in existence. That's okay. Don't be afraid to invent it yourself! Schedule a meeting with your boss every quarter and simply say, "Hey, you know what? I find that I do really well when we meet in a structured manner like this to discuss my progress." What boss worth their salt is going to say no to that?

I'll give you an example of when the company and employee's goals are well aligned. Say the company wants a major national publication to cover a new cancer breakthrough as one of their main goals for the year. Now, the person who works in the lab and runs the experiment has a clear understanding of how his or her day-to-day job contributes directly to the company goals. A nice big write up in a national publication would garner a lot of positive feelings toward the company and likely attract a lot of new clients, which in turn could lead to greater profit for the corporation. That's good for everyone.

On the flip side, imagine that the same company's number one goal for the year is to simply make a particular amount of money. (Lots of companies have this goal. And they should, or else no one would have a job.) But how is that same lab technician going to approach his experiments every day? Will he have the same level of enthusiasm and drive for success? Of course not! His job just suddenly became very monotonous and boring. And, sadly, there's now a complete disconnect between the lab technician's heart and the company's bottom line.

When the employees have a clear understanding of the company's goals, it forces them to think long and hard about whether or not it's a place they want to work. On several occasions, I have found myself in the position of working for an organization that *only* had financially related objectives. Of course, I understand that this is business, and we're all here to make money. But for the purpose of motivating the staff and making sure we have the right people on board, we need to craft better goals than this.

Many times, I have said to the board or the president, "Hey, would you consider expanding the goals of the company to three or four more so that we can create more alignment and better engagement with everybody?" I help the president understand that the solitary financial metrics do not necessarily resonate with the scientists in the trenches. The decision makers greet this suggestion with enthusiasm almost every single time. And why not? A problem has been identified and a simple solution has been presented. Everybody wins

It's the manager and the employee's job to communicate openly. The only problem is that almost nobody does this. Keep in mind that the manager's job is to manage up (suggesting that they expand the goals of the company to include his or her employees accomplishments) and manage down (ensure that his or her employees' goals are aligned with the company's).

THE "WHAT" AND THE "HOW"

There's *what* you do at work, and then there's *how* you do it. What we are talking about here with the "how" is your attitude and your behavior. Progressive companies rate both of these results during the performance evaluation process; I always say that if I ever ran my own company, that I would rate each 50/50. We all know superstar performers who alienated everyone along the way and sweet as cherry pie co-workers who never accomplished a thing.

Companies with high performing jerks oftentimes classify them as "distinguished scientists" or "individual contributors" (although, sometimes these are legitimate titles) because they basically do not play well with others. These individuals are easy to spot on an organization chart because nobody reports to them. The problem with these employees is the opportunity cost of their time in your organization. For every moment that you are enabling their bad behavior, you could have been employing a perfectly nice employee instead.

The dean of Stanford's Business School pointed this out to me when he was reviewing my department's organization chart during my business school interview. I didn't get accepted by the way because, as he informed me later, my corporation had not spent enough money there. But he did teach me about the opportunity costs of problem employees, and he also happily referred me to Santa Clara's business school program, with an essentially identical curriculum and less pricey admission requirements.

Have you ever worked for an organization that had their company values plastered up on the walls all over the place? They're there as a sort of behavior barometer to ensure that everyone gets along. They're also there so that management doesn't have to look too hard for reasons to fire the toxic people. But for the most part, no one really ever pays much attention to them.

COMMITTING TO A HAPPY "HOW"

I think there's a real opportunity to tap into those words up on the wall and use them in a more productive manner. I like to refer to the cultural values of the organization and say to the team, "Hey, can we all agree that we want to get along at work?" And they all normally say yes. And then I say, "Okay, cool. Can we then also agree that we spend way more time with each other than we spend with the loved ones in our families and in our lives?" Yes. "Can we all agree that we don't want our workplace to be a toxic situation?" Yes. "Can we all agree most importantly, you and I, that we'll use the cultural values and be honest and trust each other? We won't lie, we won't commit scientific fraud, we won't scream, we won't threaten, we won't bully, and we won't discriminate. This is what a happy work commune looks like. Can we all agree right now this is what a good *how* looks like?" And they all say yes. Who would not want this at work, right?

The next step is to say, "Now, don't be surprised. I am writing this down on a little piece of paper, which I'm going to keep in a file, stating that you have agreed with me on this date that this is what the *how* looks like. So, we all agree that if you exhibit any of these negative behaviors, you are going to be disciplined." Everyone always says yes.

But then guess what the little toxic employees do? They forget about that conversation and behave terribly, and then I have to haul their little toxic selves right back into my office and say, "Do you remember this conversation (pointing to the little piece of paper) on X date? Do you remember when we all agreed that we were going to live happily ever after in our precious little work commune? I don't think that I need to tell you which one of our cultural values you have violated today." To which they reply no and leave my office with a verbal warning. Their next infraction will garner them a written performance improvement plan (PIP). The third time that they behave poorly will likely be their last day in our happy workplace commune.

This technique works great on kids too. Both of my kids signed contracts with acceptable behavioral norms that were mutually agreed upon in advance when they were teenagers. The associated punishments were also agreed upon in advance. As soon as they misbehaved, there was no screaming, yelling, or drama; I simply pulled out their precious little contracts and reminded them of the content. The most important part in all of this is that both parties agree upon everything in advance when everyone is sane and rational. And guess who you should let lead this process during its creation? Them!

I asked my adult son to prepare his own contract when I left him home alone while I vacationed in Italy for two weeks. The contract stated that he would not have any parties at my house while I was away, and if he did, then he would not be allowed to live in my house anymore. Well, sure enough, he had a big party, and I just so happened to call right in the middle of it. Gotta love the universe, huh? And as soon as he heard my voice on the other end of the line, he said, "Mom, I'm packing!" He moved himself out of my house by the time I landed back in the US.

GIVE POWER, GET RESULTS

A lot of the successes and transformations I have witnessed or have been a catalyst for come from giving the power to others, or quite simply, letting them lead. There is nothing more demoralizing or energy zapping than being micromanaged to death. A clock-watching manager who scolds you if you're a few minutes late is not empowering his staff to act for themselves. Little things like this add up over time and leave you feeling miserable.

Personally, I don't care what time people come in or what time they leave as long as they get their work done and they're engaged while they're there (keep in mind that most of my employees are exempt, which means that they do not punch time cards and they are paid to perform a job, rather than collect an hourly rate). This is about trusting and empowering people to manage their own time; they're not a pack of kindergarteners. People don't understand that if you give the power away, it comes back in spades every single time.

CHAPTER 5

EVERY MOMENT IS A CHOICE

YOU MAY HAVE NOTICED THAT EVERYTHING IN THIS book so far depends on making a choice for yourself, and choosing your attitude is no different.

TEACHING PEOPLE HOW TO TREAT YOU

Sometimes the very worst situations are the best learning opportunities. I'll use myself as the example for this one.

I once worked with a woman who was unquestionably a toxic boss. She freaked out on numerous occasions, and the first time it happened, I was really upset. We've all been there, right? She went crazy on me: screaming and yelling and telling me how unhappy she was with my performance. Now, please bear in mind that I had not done anything wrong.

Regardless, I allowed myself to be incredibly upset by her toxic behavior.

At some point later that night, I had a conversation with myself about the situation. The conversation went something like this, "Am I going to let this situation bring me up, or am I going to let this drive me down? What is my plan for this toxic boss woman? Do I want to continue allowing her to treat me this way? Am I just going to take it and essentially teach her that it's okay to treat me like this?" No!

A few weeks later (it's always good to give yourself some time to calm down from an unpleasant situation), I made an appointment with her (face to face is best, but she was located in another country). I let her know that when she went off on me—screaming and yelling, etc.—it really hurt my feelings, and that I wished she would stop doing this to me. I respectfully asked her to please gather more information in the future before unleashing what felt like a tornado of her emotions on me. A few "when you do X, it hurts my feelings" sentences later, I think she finally heard me because she never yelled at me, or anyone else that I know of, ever again.

HOW TO SAY NO TO UNWANTED BEHAVIOR

Luckily, there is a perfectly legal, relatively easy, and straightforward four-step process to reversing unwanted behavior in the workplace. If you follow these steps, whoever is bothering you will cease doing so, and you won't even have to involve HR!

Position the discussion in a manner such that you are providing someone with feedback. Remember, this is a 50/50 relationship, and you always need to meet the other person in the middle. So, here are the four steps:

1. Ask the person if they are okay with receiving some feedback about the exchange you two recently shared. If the person says "no," well then, game over, and you will likely need to involve HR, unfortunately. In most situations, however, he or she will say yes.

2. State the facts. "I saw you in the hall, and you were in a huge hurry. Remember?"

3. State how the interaction made you feel. Focus on the behavior and do not get into name calling. "When you were in a hurry, you cut me off mid-sentence, and that made me feel really bad." When positioned in this way, the other person could never come back and say that you are wrong, because you are talking about your *feelings*. Your feelings cannot be judged as wrong.

4. Ask an open-ended question. "Can you understand how that behavior could have hurt?"

This process almost always leads to an apology, unless the other person is a complete jerk with zero regard for anyone else's feelings. Of course, people like that do exist, but nine times out of ten this four-step process will help clear the air. Most people never speak up when something is bothering them, and then the ill will just festers. This is a fast and effective way to have an uncomfortable discussion that leads to resolution; it's a *courageous* way to approach a difficult conversation.

The important thing with this process is to schedule the conversation; don't do it in the moment. Wait at least twenty-four hours to talk about whatever is bothering you so that the immediacy of your feelings can dissipate a little bit, and you're not walking into the discussion all fired up. I can assure you that most times, the person never intended to hurt your feelings. More importantly, the behavior that bothered you will stop. This is an important part of teaching people how to treat you. You need to stop and take a minute to let them know that their behavior impacts your feelings in a negative way. This process works wonders on bullies. Try it and see.

And before I forget, I do not suggest dragging HR into these situations. In cases like this, no good deed goes unpunished. Involving HR will not work in your favor, and besides, there are more effective ways of handling things on your own. Oftentimes, that one simple sentence of "when you did or said X, it hurt my feelings" does the trick. The entire point of choosing your attitude is to take your power back. By not allowing someone to crush your emotions, you are regaining control over the situation. You are not letting the situation own you; you are leading the situation yourself.

PRESSURE MAKES DIAMONDS

When someone hands you a bunch of lemons, what do you

do with them? Make lemonade, of course! It's all in how you frame the problem for yourself and how you articulate the solution (to yourself and others) that determines how the situation will impact you.

Say you mess something up at work. For example, an experiment that you've been working on setting up for months backfires, and it's basically your fault. We've all been there, and it can be pretty crushing. But if you look at this experience as a reference point, a learning experience, and a good example of what not to do next time, you can easily chose to turn a failure into a success. Take the emotions out of it and use the experience as a data point. This is called a failure analysis, and don't forget that you learn the most from the worst.

If you find yourself in a scenario where you have screwed up in a major way, a lot of the damage can be undone by simply owning up to your mistake. All you need to do is approach the appropriate person and say, "Joe, I totally screwed up the experiment. I wanted to be the first to tell you. I've taken a gigantic step back and assessed the damage, and I've come up with an improvement plan for next time." Intention a positive outcome for yourself, and you'll be surprised at the response you get. It sure beats saying, "You know what, Joe? I just messed up that really expensive experiment we've been working on for the last few months. I wouldn't be surprised if you had to let me go." Or worse yet, trying to cover up your mistake by playing dumb or blaming someone else for your mistake. That strategy will get you nowhere fast!

How you own your reaction and how you let it affect you emotionally is 100% on you. Take a note from the Millennials; when something undesirable happens, they say, "My bad." Those two little words make a world of difference. They mean, "I screwed up, I'm sorry, and I'll fix it."

It's all in how you respond. Have you ever seen the TED Talk with Kelly McGonigal about stress?[4] She says, and she is absolutely dead on, that stress can either drive you to an early grave or it can make you better and stronger. I always say that pressure makes diamonds, because it's true. There are very few work scenarios in which we just blissfully float along without a moment's worry or concern. Where is the challenge in that? Being at work is not intended to be a walk in the park. If you think that pressure and stress will cause you to have a heart attack, then you could very well have one. But if you think that stress makes you think faster and respond in a more a thoughtful way, then you will shine brighter.

But let's be fair. An unhealthy (this is going to shave the ends off of your telomeres regardless of what you think about it) level of stress is not what we're talking about here. In these situations, I suggest that you speak with your feet and find a healthier day job. Life is way too short to let your job shorten your precious minutes on this planet.

4   http://www.ted.com/talks/
     kelly_mcgonigal_how_to_make_stress_your_friend?language=en

GROUPTHINK

You're not alone in all of this either. It is the responsibility of management to create an environment in which employees feel safe to fail. Humans are not perfect, and mistakes happen all the time. If people are not permitted the space to voice a dissenting opinion, or to admit their mistakes, then everyone is drinking the Kool-Aid and potentially dangerous situations can arise quickly. Even in a Command-and-Control leadership situation, there must be some wiggle room for positive dissension.

Think about the horrible moment in our history when NASA's space shuttle blew up. No one listened to what the consultants were saying, and everyone was too afraid to address the elephant in the living room. This happened not once, but twice! It wasn't a safe environment to fail in, to be wrong, or to have a different opinion at all. This is called "groupthink," and it's not healthy. Check out the groupthink learning regarding the shuttle disasters online; it's fascinating and sad at the same time. And once you have learned to spot groupthink from a distance, all of a sudden you will notice it everywhere.

NEGOTIATE LIKE THE BOYS DO

Finding your heart is a massive leap forward, but it's not enough. You need to speak it out loud and make yourself heard. We hear a lot about wage inequality in the workplace, and it's not because women deserve less or do less. It's because we don't demand it like the boys have learned to do. The boys are off negotiating while we're sitting at Starbucks bitching about it. I've seen this happen so many times.

Sally says, "Oh, thank you so much for offering me this great job for $50,000. That's amazing. Thank you. Yes, I'd love to accept your offer!" Along comes Charlie, and he says, "Oh, you want me for $50,000? That's nice, but there's just no way that I can make that work. I can't do it for less than $60,000, and I would like a $2,500 sign on bonus to offset the year-end bonus that I will not receive this year. I am also going to need you to buy me out of my unvested stock options as well." And he gets all of this! Women need to up the ante and play the game the exact same way the boys do. And guess where I learned this? The boys! We need to attach our mouths to our hearts and go out and negotiate! (I've actually taught these tactics to a fair number of boys who hadn't learned them from their guy friends.)

YOUR HERD AT WORK

A big part of rocking the *how* is taking a close look at *who* you are hanging out with. We talked about this when I introduced the concept of hiring your own personal board of directors, but I think it's important to give careful thought to everyone in your life and how they are impacting it. Are you surrounded by a group of Debbie Downers who are always complaining? Are you choosing to surround yourself with givers or takers? A lot of times, the negative, toxic people are right under your very own roof.

Who are you choosing to have in your life? We have another data collecting opportunity with this one! Map yourself and the people you come into contact with over any given week. What are these people doing to enrich your life or help make you better? Can you pin point a person or people who bring you down when you're in their company? Every single relationship, not just the one with your boss, is *your* choice. Vote for yourself and get rid of the energy suckers. Just because you happen to be related to the person doesn't mean that you need to give them permission to suck you dry and zap your momentum. I am constantly amazed at the number of parents with perfectly capable 30-something-year-old "children" who are still sitting on their parent's couch, munching on orange Cheetos and watching their parent's big screen TV day in and day out—because they chose to let them!

We only have so many minutes on this earth, and you get to choose how you spend virtually every single one of them. Every minute that you spend with a beautifully loving, giving, and cheerfully partnered employee or co-worker is another minute that you are not giving to a toxic bully taker. Make a change; forget regret. It's your choice; you're in control.

I'm from the Silicon Valley, and I know a lot of serial entrepreneurs and venture capitalists. I was having lunch with a VC friend of mine recently, and he told me that one of his benchmarks for investing in someone is how the person seeking funding treats the waiter at the pitch lunch. You can tell so much about a person simply by how they interact with someone in the service industry. Do they smile? Make eye contact? Engage in a full exchange? Use "please" and "thank you"? Do they exhibit the basics of human interaction and kindness? So many people do not take the time to be polite and courteous, and if that's the case, according to my friend, they won't get a dime of his money. If someone is going to act like that at lunch, how are they going to behave back at the office?

My friend was able to make the connection between being courteous and being able to lead. You can't have one without the other. Many hiring managers make their decisions the same way by simply taking the candidate out to lunch and seeing how they interact with the waiter. Who you let in to your herd and how each person is treated matters significantly.

THE DRAMA TRIANGLE

On day one, and at the same time that I teach people the importance of loving themselves first (because nobody else will), I lay out my emphatic intolerance for drama of any kind. Behaving like a drama queen or king is a fireable offense in my book. I make this clear right up front, during the conversation in which we all agree that we want to work in a pleasant environment. Of course, nobody would ever admit that they are a drama king or queen, because honestly, most people aren't even aware of the proverbial crown that rests atop their heads. Nevertheless, I don't want drama at work. End of story. This is not negotiable.

The drama triangle has, as you might have guessed, three 60-degree angled points: the hero, the persecutor, and the victim. You can easily learn more about this concept online, and I encourage you to do so.

I spend at least fifteen minutes with my new employees individually to discuss the drama triangle topic. I ask them if they recognize anyone in their own family with one of the three characteristics. Have they ever worked for someone who fits the profile? Do they recognize these traits in their co-workers, friends, former bosses, or themselves? Speak up now, because I will not have a hero, persecutor, or villain working in our communal midst. Drama is not productive; it's not healthy; it's not nice; it's simply not tolerated. I ask every new employee if they would like to work in a drama-free workplace, and they all say yes!

Admittedly, I do go a little nuts when it comes to this, but I firmly believe that you should take this seriously. Drama spreads quickly and can bring the whole team crashing down in no time. What's interesting, and what can also be slightly terrifying, is that the three personality points of the drama triangle often do some shape shifting to add to an already confusing and heightened emotional situation. Every selfishly anointed drama king or queen normally reigns supremely with a primary and also a secondary role that they prefer to play.

Here's an example. There was an initiative to teach people how to conduct a new molecular test at one of my companies. The instructor on this project was a bully/persecutor. If he didn't like you, he wouldn't select you to be a part of the learned next group. He made people wait an interminable amount of time to be a part of his class. By the time he did select a handful of people, he then became a hero in their eyes, all while they became victims in their own minds. They felt unworthy and worried that they would never be able to grasp the material. The hero in some ways became the rescuer, because at last, he was going to share his knowledge with others and elevate them to his status. It was all a very delicate and complicated mind game, which the end result was nothing but damage: damage to morale, damage to the team spirit, and damage to employee confidence. (Not to mention a colossal waste of time, energy, and resources.)

This guy, teacher/persecutor/hero, was nothing more than the elephant in the living room who had not been properly managed by his boss who came before me. When people behave like this, they are immediately given a verbal warning (after signing that little piece of paper and understanding our cultural norms, including what the drama triangle is). Just think of how much more peaceful your daily existence at work would be if your boss had the guts to tackle the drama triangle. Most people don't even know what the drama triangle is in the first place because they have never been outside of it long enough to see it from a strategic perspective. I expect that if any of my employees see even a hint or whisper of a drama triangle unfolding, they call each other on it right away. What am I teaching them to do here? They are all learning how to have the guts to deal with the leadership of a team out and away from the drama triangle on their own!

PLUS, DELTA

Beyond all of the kumbaya (don't "K" words rock?) tactics that most people associate me with, I am also really big on metrics. I'm a scientist after all, and looking at things analytically, from a data perspective, was reinforced in business school as well. To that end, there is a scientific way to measure people's attitudes, and I do that by asking a series of questions. In my one-on-one meetings where I'm checking in with people to gauge how they are doing, at the end, I just step up to the white board and fire away.

- What's going well here? These are the "pluses."
- What's not going well here? These are the "deltas." What a nice way of saying the "negatives," huh? :)
- What could be improved? These are our "next steps."

The end sum of this exercise gives you a pretty good idea of where things stand with that particular employee. Interestingly, these three simple questions are all that you really ever need to ask on surveys as well.

This approach can also be used in a team setting, and it's an effective way to take the pulse of the group at the end of an event. In a group setting, it's sometimes called "courageous feedback." What a nice way of giving you permission to share everything, huh? Generally, people are afraid to be the first ones to speak up, particularly if what they have to say is less than positive. But all it takes is one person to get the ball rolling, and it helps tremendously if that person has chosen their attitude. Opening the floor to an ocean of complaints isn't productive, but identifying problems and suggesting solutions are absolutely productive.

ACTIVE LISTENING

Sometimes, the most important thing that you can choose to do in the workplace is to shut up and actively listen. Active listening is the art of genuinely paying attention with intent. With the advent of everyone bringing their cell phones, tablets, and/or laptops with them to meetings, and actually having the nerve to use them right in front of their co-workers during face-to-face meetings, active listening is becoming even more important. By simply *not* looking at your phone or laptop during a meeting, you will be ahead of the curve.

Active listening can be performed with a number of your senses; in addition to simply being quiet, not speaking, and looking at the speaker, your interest can be conveyed to the speaker by nodding your head and smiling or agreeing by saying "Yes" or simply "Mmm hmm" to encourage them to continue. You can also paraphrase back to them what they said, e.g., "So, what I heard you say is x, y, and z. Is that correct?"

Active listening, as my many repeated 360-degree feedback exercises have reminded me over the years, is not my greatest strength. :) And for additional learning on the active listening subject, I am going to have to refer you to where else but YouTube and/or the Internet! :)

CHAPTER 6

HIRING GIVERS AND FIRING TAKERS

LETTING THEM INTERVIEW

WHEN I'M NEW TO A JOB AND FIRST ENCOUNTER THE team, it's likely that they have not gelled yet. Everyone is still a little frazzled and unfocused. I do not want people who are in this state of mind involved with interviewing external job applicants because the internal toxicity level may still be very high (the bad apples are likely still in place). The team is not yet speaking with one unified voice, and just one toxic person could lead to a disaster in an interview situation. I've seen companies put their most toxic employees on the front lines of interviewing, and the results are not pretty. Why would anyone put their Negative Nancy in charge of recruiting? Where is the sense in that? It blows my mind.

So, imagine, I'm six or eight months in and the people who are left on the team are all there because they really, truly, deep down, all want to be there. I am left with a team of givers, for the most part. Everyone has normed, and they are speaking with one voice. Their hearts are aligned with the company's mission, and everyone is humming along in unison, discovering the rewards of working with a team of similarly minded and driven individuals. It's a beautiful thing when this happens, and now, finally, they are ready to participate in the interviewing process.

THE $500 QUESTION

Once I have my team operating in synch, they take care of the majority of the screening process and the bulk of the interviewing. They spearhead the team interviews in which the candidate is invited to come in and have lunch. The mood is generally really festive and positive, the team talks about how well they all get along, and the cool work they are doing. At this point, they've been taught the legal dos and don'ts, they've been coached similarly (in a safe environment), and I trust them to take care of the technical side of each applicant's qualifications as a team; they do the bulk of the legwork. I let them lead, after all.

Most of the time, I meet with the candidate for only fifteen to twenty minutes after the team has been through their initial set of questions. When I sit down with the candidate, I usually ask them what brought them to our company and this position in particular. Eventually, I ask, "Imagine, David, that today is your lucky day. With the best of intentions, I.m going to hire you. What if, two months from now, I call you into my office and give you $500 in $20s and the rest of the day off. What would you do with the money, and what would you do with the time?"

The responses are unbelievably revealing. You can tell within one nanosecond if the person is a giver or a taker. If the person is a taker they don't stop for a single pause before launching into how they would spend the money on themselves; they always answer the money question first. I've heard some pretty creative responses, but still, if the person is a taker, they don't hesitate an iota or give a thought to anyone else. One guy immediately replied, "In five minutes, I'd be at the mall, and I'd buy fourteen videos for $500, and then I'd go home and play video games all by myself, all day long." And I said, "So, do you play the kind of games where you are connected to other players around the world?" And he said, "Oh, no. I only play against myself." Needless to say, this guy did not get hired. It's shocking what people will say because they're so caught off guard.

Now that I am sharing my secret giver/taker screening question in this book, I may never be able to ask it again. I have already dealt with one or two candidates who had been tipped off by one of the few takers on the team that had yet to leave the roost. I'll share my favorite "faker taker" story because it's a really good one.

This gal came in for the interview, and I asked her my screening question just like always. Only this time, it was so obvious to me that she was prepared for the question. Her immediate response was, "Oh my. Well, give me a second. Hmmm, you know I;ve heard that everybody works in the laboratory here, and I can't imagine all of you standing on your feet all day long. If I had $500, I would take the money, and I would go measure everyone's feet. Then I'd go straight to CVS and buy Dr. Scholl's shoe inserts for every single person on the team. You know what? I'm not sure if $500 would be enough, so I might need to ask for a little bit more money. Is that okay?" I find this hysterical because you cannot *lie about who you are*. Please! I can usually tell when people appear to be too good to be true. This gal was beyond fake, and she didn't get hired either.

The responses that catch my attention and make my own heart melt are ones that express a true spirit of generosity. These answers are sometimes just as unbelievable and have a more positive outcome for everyone. Some of my favorites are:

- "Wait, am I the only one who gets the money and the day off?" Hired. This person immediately thought about everyone else.
- "I don't want to leave the team with my newfound fortune alone. Can everyone else please come with me?" Hired. Team mentality.
- "I would go make a nice picnic lunch for everybody and then bring it back to them." Hired. Giver.
- "I would give you a hug and thank you and ask you if you had any plans for dinner later that night." Hired. This person thought about me instead of herself!

You can tell immediately that these people care about others. Their gut reaction is to share and contribute to the greater good of everyone in the group. I don't have anything against people who play video games or even who try to gain the upper hand, but what separates a giver from a taker is their initial, split second response to how they would handle an unexpected gift of money and time.

My third question "What do you do for fun?" is equally telling. The response indicates where they are in their life. What I am really asking is "Where does your heart lead you?" You never know where the person is heading until they answer this question. The response gives you extra data points: Are they pulled toward isolation, adventure, group activities, or intellectual endeavors?

There is a fourth way that I identify givers or takers during the hiring process, and it's something we touched on earlier: the importance of interviewing back. How does this come into play? As I mentioned, most of the time people don't interview back, and they are missing a huge opportunity for themselves. But there are the rare few that do. The takers are easy to spot again because they initially ask questions primarily about themselves or the job as it relates to them. For example: How much money am I going to make? What time am I expected to be here every morning? How much time off will I have? That kind of thing. Whereas the givers always ask about team moral and what their opportunities will be to contribute. It's just so interesting to me how cut and dry people are. There is very little middle ground, and the types are so easy to spot. It's all a matter of learning the language of the takers versus the givers.

I was talking about interviewing practices with a recruiter friend the other day, and he had a really interesting spin on this topic. He said that he always asks people what they do for fun. If they don't respond with something competitive, then he won't refer them. This means that he is recruiting primarily for Type A, adventurous personalities, which makes sense because he is evaluated on the quality of his referrals for hire. Alternatively, I am judged on the quality of my commune, or the strength of our team, and teams function better with givers predominating.

As crazy as this might sound, working with a team of givers is kind of like being in a church congregation. There are all different types of people and multiple personalities inside a church, but everyone is there for the same reason. They have a common purpose. They're there to give something with their hearts and their souls. It's a beautiful, wonderful, powerful thing. They are there to give, they all come together, and they leave fulfilled. Going to work should feel like that. Why not?

One cute postscript about givers and takers. I tried to give Adam Grant, the author of the bestselling book *Give and Take: Why Helping Others Drives Our Success*, this $500 question idea for his next book (I had heard that he was looking for methods of sorting out givers and takers), and he wouldn't take it. Why? It dawned on me after we exchanged a few, super nice emails back and forth. Because he is such a giver, he wouldn't take it. At one point, I remember thinking, "I just might have to write my own book and tell everyone about my $500 question myself." :)

A DAMNED GOOD FIRE

An HR colleague of mine once said, "The only thing better than a good hire is a damned good fire." Firing is a necessity of good leadership. There is no way around it. When I first started out, I was horrified at the prospect, but over time, I have come to view the firing process as just that, a process. It doesn't have to be painful for either party. In fact, if you treat the other person with the utmost respect, it is highly feasible that they will leave with their dignity and self-worth fully intact. They will likely even feel *good* about leaving. When executed correctly, firing someone can actually be an extremely positive experience.

The highest return on investment that a manager can make is getting rid of dead weight within the organization. There is scientific data that proves this theory, and it's one of the core teachings in business school. You know who they are, those rotten apples, and you can almost spot them from a mile away. They are like gigantic boulders in a stream, and everyone else is the water trying to get around them. To bring true value to the team, the best thing that management can do is wade in there and remove those boulders so that everyone else can flow merrily along their way.

One of the best questions that you can ask in an interview to gauge both the boss and the organization is "When was the last time you fired someone?" If the boss has never fired anyone, contrary to the harmony it may indicate, this is a bad sign. It means that he or she may tolerate mediocrity within their organization and are perfectly content to just let it sit and fester indefinitely.

Not only must you trust your boss to hire and nurture good, giving, and strong people, but you should also be able to expect that they will get rid of the toxic employees. This is not too much to anticipate from a healthy, functioning organization. You're all in the same commune together. Can you trust your boss or upper management to get rid of the bad fruit? Keeping the commune peaceful is a core responsibility for management.

If you ask anyone what stresses them out the most at work, 85-90% of the people surveyed will say that it's their toxic, taking boss. It's the number one reason people leave their jobs. This all goes back to the culture that you are choosing for yourself. You spend anywhere between fifty to eighty hours with these people a week, and it is critical that you can rely on the individuals on your team to be kind, cheerful, partnered, and collaborative. It's a lot easier to pick your boss than it is to pick the entire team around you; however, if you choose wisely on the boss, chances are strong that he or she will have the know-how to assemble a good team.

The firing process is actually quite simple. I get to know my employees first. I find out what makes them tick, what drives them, and I challenge them to find and live their hearts. That piece alone usually causes a good majority of people to leave on their own accord. They do some digging and discover that their hearts are not aligned with the company's vision, and off they go to find the thing that does drive them. Everybody wins. Instead of firing people, I encourage them to seek opportunities that are a better fit and, as a result, will be significantly more rewarding for them. On many occasions, believe it or not, the people who leave remain close professional colleagues of mine. Thank you, LinkedIn.

Let's say that John is well on a path to separation (by the way, "separation" from the company is used more commonly than "being fired" these days). Now, I am presupposing that some of the important introductory steps have been followed (as discussed in chapter four), but here's how it normally goes:

Me: "Hey, John. Do you remember when I hired you, we agreed that we didn't want any drama here in the workplace?"

John: ""Yeah."

Me: "I even have this documented. See here. If you got into the drama triangle, I was going to first give you a verbal warning and then PIP you if you did not improve after the verbal warning.""

John: "Yep. I remember." (We all remember chapter One, right?)

Me: "Okay, John. So, this is really simple. You exhibited X, Y, and Z behavior recently, all of which is not what we agreed on back in September of last year. I gave you a verbal warning in November (also documented), and now I am giving you a written warning/Performance Improvement Plan. This should not be a surprise to you because we agreed on accepted behaviors, and you even signed this piece of paper. If you do this again, we're going to go to the next level of disciplinary action, which is that you will be terminated. Are you okay with this?"

Of course, John will say that he is okay with this step, sign the piece of paper, promise to change, and then be on his way. He may initially try to explain his way out of the scenario, but he knows that the facts are the facts. Will John change? Will he stop engaging in drama triangles and terrorizing others? Of course not. People don't change (for the most part), especially toxic people. But what I have done is essentially gave him the inner strength from which he will separate himself from the company. I am not the one engaging in toxic behavior. He is. It's only a matter of time and company policy before John goes from bad to gone.

We have been clear about expectations from day one, and he agreed to them. Every organization has different rules and regulations about how many warnings a person should be given before they are terminated, so be sure to always follow their procedures/protocols—and here is where I strongly recommend that you partner very closely with HR long before you give John the verbal warning. The toxic people who really need to be fired simply continue to be toxic. And as a manager, you just let them do it. By the time all of their violations have stacked up, almost every single time, the person will say, "Hand me the papers to sign. I'll be on my way."

Just like when my son moved out of my house of his own fruition. There's no drama, there's no fighting, and there are no surprises. If there are any surprises, it's my bad as a manager. I screwed up somewhere along the path and was not clear about my expectations and the company's expectations. You are simply treating people the way you would want to be treated. The rules have been agreed upon in advance. You have taught them about the behaviors that will be accepted, and there is zero ambiguity. They have violated the rules, and you are helping them to fire themselves. As in everything I do, I let them lead themselves.

It's important to note that I do not label or judge John as a "bad employee." Rather, John and the company were a bad fit together. It's John's behaviors that caused the issue, and it's John's behaviors that have allowed me, as the manager, to help him lead himself down the path of separation.

Because of this "no surprises" approach, I can happily say that I have never had a bad fire. I don't even know how many people I have helped to fire themselves, but I have never been sued or had to go to mediation because there have never been any surprises. It's not personal, and in every single case, everyone has been better off almost immediately.

And one postscript about people changing. I will never forget sitting in the drive-through line at McDonald's with my cardiologist boyfriend and hearing him exclaim, "Oh my gosh, Michaela. I just put three stents in that guy's heart two weeks ago after his near life-ending heart attack, and here he is back at McDonald's ordering two Big Macs for dinner!" Uh

yeah—people don't really change the core of who they are...
that much!

SAVING FACE

When you treat people with honor, good things happen. I
learned this from my ex-husband who is a cop. (He and I were
not a good "fit" either, but that's a story for another book.) I
was driving home from work one night, and I saw the blue
flashing lights on the side of the road. Back in the day, I always
worried that it would be my ex-husband behind those lights,
and in this case, it was. He had pulled someone over, and
they were in what looked like a full on fistfight on the side of
the road. It took me a minute to register that my Rambo-like,
hunk of a husband was fielding punches like that from someone who he was obviously trying to subdue. I pulled over to
watch out of his sight. The punches kept coming, and I was
starting to get worried. There was a small crowd of people
looking on, and no one was doing anything to intervene.

After what seemed like a very long time, the altercation
settled down a little bit. Suddenly, the guy became very
docile, stopped throwing punches, and quietly and agreeably
allowed my ex to calmly cuff him and put him into the back
of the police cruiser. I was stunned by the whole interaction,
and I couldn't understand why my ex didn't just shove him
in the back of the car once he had finally calmed down. I
headed home and waited for my husband to arrive. When
he got home, I told him I had seen the whole thing but could
not, for the life of me, understand why he let the guy punch
him like that.

He just said, "Oh, Michaela, that whole scene was orchestrated. It was one big charade. We had made a deal amongst ourselves and that fight scene was a big part of it." What? He explained that this guy wasn't just being taken down to the station for questioning; he was being arrested for his third strike, and thus, he was going to prison for a long time. If he was going to have any chance of staying alive on the inside, he needed to "save face" on the outside. The missed punches and the crowds were all part of allowing this guy to show his fellow gang members who were watching that he was a tough criminal. My ex explained that if this guy hadn't been allowed to "save face" like that, he would have probably been killed when he got to prison.

What does this cop story have to do with firing toxic people at work? Well, letting people save face is an easy way to avoid a potentially dangerous situation. We've all heard about the disgruntled employee who shows up at the workplace with a gun and goes on a shooting rampage, but there are less newsworthy incidents that happen over work disputes every single day. Just because something doesn't make the evening news, doesn't make it any less scary or dangerous.

LET THEM RESIGN INSTEAD

There is a significantly safer way to handle a potentially volatile situation and thereby hedge workplace violence. You cannot cut people off or isolate them or very bad things will happen. This is why giving people the power to control their own destinies is so important. They do the work themselves, and everything is significantly more peaceful, right down to the final moments.

When the person knows they are well on a path to being fired, I simply ask them if they would like to resign instead, thus allowing them to save face. While they may not be able to collect unemployment benefits, I let them resign if that's what they would prefer. Again, even in this moment, I'm letting them lead. The dignity that this path affords them is very much appreciated and void of drama. They oftentimes thank me and give me a hug for they would have never thought of this option on their own. Also, this allows them to tell future employers that they resigned, instead of mentioning that they were fired. More oftentimes than not, we are simply dealing with a bad "fit," not bad employees.

QUITTING IS OKAY

Just the other day, I was asked to lunch by a former employee who wanted to speak to me about a toxic workplace that she had allowed herself to experience for the past three years. She realized that this workplace was poisoning her, but she did not want to quit because she thought that quitting was a bad thing. I asked her two very simple questions. First, "Do you feel like you are in a toxic prison?" She said, "Yes, that is exactly what it feels like." And then I said, "Why are you judging yourself so negatively for letting yourself out of a toxic prison?" She had never thought about quitting like this. All that I needed to do for her was to create a safe environment for her to care for herself and give her permission to put herself ahead of her corporation. Sometimes what people really need to do is simply love and lead themselves.

CHAPTER 7

YOUR COMMUNE AT WORK

MOST OF US SPEND WAY MORE TIME AT WORK THAN WE do anywhere else, and (sadly) we spend more time with our work colleagues than we do our loved ones. Our co-workers are our daytime families in essence. They are our commune at work. I looked up the definition of commune when I first started using this term (to make sure that it didn't have some crazy religious meaning), and I found the following definition: "a group of people living together and sharing possessions and responsibilities." Perfect! We need to work on maintaining our commune at work and paying very close attention to who comes into it. All relationships require work, and our communal work relationships are absolutely no different.

I interviewed a very kind woman the other day who described the new team that we were attempting to build as follows: "Wow, Michaela. It's like we are all going to be going to the moon together, and we are deciding who gets to come on the rocket ship!" Thus, for my latest company, we are going to call it a rocket ship instead of a commune. :)

Luckily, there is no shortage of activities to serve you in this endeavor. When I first introduce some of these ideas, it should come as no surprise that people look at me like I am a tad bit crazy. I anticipate the sideways glances and even get a kick out of them most of the time. Why? Because I know this stuff works, as crazy as it may seem, no matter how uptight the scientific environment is that I am in.

MIRROR, MIRROR, ROCK STAR ON THE WALL

Have you ever walked into a molecular or diagnostic laboratory (or any workplace for that matter) and seen a mirror on the wall? And no, I am not talking about in the bathroom; I am talking about in the laboratory proper, where the laboratorians actually work. Odds are pretty strong that you haven't. Labs are usually, by necessity, sterile environments with everything in its place and just so. One of the things I do upon arrival is a little redecorating by hanging mirrors in a few strategic locations. People need to look at themselves and see who is staring back at them. It's part of loving yourself.

It doesn't stop there though. I personally believe we all have a little rock star inside of us, jamming on his or her guitar, belting out lyrics to swooning fans, and just generally killing it. Not long ago, it occurred to me that I could take the mirror identity loving thing a step further (always pushing) and get stickers (in purple, the company's favorite corporate color) that actually say, "I'm a rock star!" and place them on the mirrors in the labs (like I did the mirror in my bedroom). I enlisted the help of our colleague in procurement, who knew just where to find the stickers that I had in mind. I was originally thinking plain black, but he was the one who deserves all of the credit for ordering the stickers in purple and in a rocking font, complete with an exclamation point too! This is a great example of a 1+1=10 situation, for what he and I both created together was even better for this situation.

I then instructed all of the employees to stand in front of those mirrors every day, put their arms up high over their heads, and proudly proclaim, "I'm a rock star!" They saw me walking around, throwing my hands up in the air, and yelling, "I'm a rock star!" They all looked at me and rolled their eyes and thought that I was nuts. But I didn't care! I simply kept doing it—and was thus creating a safe environment for them to start doing it too!

A few weeks after the stickers were applied to the mirrors, we hired William; he's a really smart kid from UCLA. Not long after our procurement guy installed the mirrors and decorated them with stickers, William sent an email to the whole team titled, "Michaela is NOT crazy!" He wrote, "I think we really should listen to Michaela, for her crazy rock star put your arms up in front of the new mirrors stuff really works! It's legit!" William had discovered a TED Talk by social scientist, Amy Cuddy, about the importance of body language and how it can literally shape your life.[5] Ah, YouTube validation yet again; it saves me every time. Thanks, William!

Laughter really is the best medicine, and it's infectious too. This kumbaya lovefest with the mirrors and the stickers and the rock star salutations has a tendency to catch on like wildfire. I suggest to my employees that they do it once a day, and you would not believe what a difference it makes. What starts as a big joke and an opportunity for everyone to make fun of me quickly turns into a conversation piece. People come by our lab on special tours just to see my employees dressed in their white lab coats, wearing their purple latex gloves, dancing in front of the mirror with their arms up over the heads, and saying to each other, "I'm a rock star! No, *you're* a rock star! Hey, let's start a rock band!" The next thing you know people are taking selfies in the mirror and posting the pictures all over the place. I've seen vendors take selfies, and people from other departments, because everyone wants in.

TAKE BACK THE MEETING

Have you ever heard of a commune having a leader? No, I'm not talking about the Moonies or the Mansons. This is a *commune*, not a *cult*. And the clear lack of hierarchy is just one of the many important differentiators. At our weekly staff meetings, we sit (equally) at a round table, and everyone participates. I purposefully do not sit at the head of the table. Even though I am the boss, every person takes turns

5   http://www.ted.com/talks/
    amy_cuddy_your_body_language_shapes_who_you_are?language=en

leading the staff meetings. It brings a fresh perspective to the group and is a challenge for each individual. It also goes to show them that I mean it when I tell them that I am going to teach them to lead.

Every week a different person is the note taker; everyone gets an equal voice and equal floor time. We do not let an eager beaver steal the floor week after week either. Action items are followed up on, we're getting oxygen to the brain, and it's a short opportunity for everyone to come together and share as equals. We're energized, feeling social, and ready to crank out some work. My new team has named this time together, "Mondays with Michaela!" They clearly have not learned yet that it's eventually going to be much more about *them* and significantly less about me.

I personally try to keep the subjects different and new so that all of the employees remain engaged in the process. It's amazing what you learn about each other when you give everyone the chance to lead in a baby step and very safe environment. At the end of the meetings, one employee mentions a random fact just for fun; the employee responsible for the random fact changes from meeting to meeting as well. Once each employee has mastered one technique (e.g., random fact giver, lunch organizer, minute taker, leader, etc.), I ask them to step it up a notch to the next level of meeting leadership. If the group gets sophisticated enough, we'll conduct the meetings standing up, which teaches people to focus and also makes the meetings a lot shorter, say ten to fifteen minutes.

STORMING/FORMING/NORMING/PERFORMING

When you bring people together from different herds and communes, they have to go through a unifying process together, or they'll be out of synch forever. We've touched on this earlier when we talked about hiring and firing in chapter six. When I first encounter the team that I am going to work with, everyone is out of whack. They lack unity and they are not speaking with a singular voice. To get them to a place where they are able to function as a cohesive unit, we all go through a systematic storming/forming/norming/ performing process to get on the same page.

This team development system was developed in 1965 by Bruce Tuckman, an educational psychologist at Ohio State who is well known in group management circles. *Storming* is like a herd of animals all running into each other. There is no order, there are no commonalities, and everything is pretty chaotic. After a small bit of time, alphas rise to the top and start organizing through *forming* small groups within the larger group. A little more time goes by, and they start *norming* in that they have created an identity for themselves. They are no longer a rambling collection of individuals. They have come together as a collective unit with a common drive. Then, once they have normed, they are all in step, they have one voice, and they can start *performing* together as a team. A great synopsis of this can be found on, where else? YouTube![6]

Most people need to be taught about this process before we launch into it, and it serves as a point of reference for

6   https://www.youtube.com/watch?v=nFE8IaoInQU

the progress they have made. When my team says, "Hey, Michaela. How come we're not interviewing people for that new lab technician spot?" I can respond by saying, "Because we're still *forming*. We're not quite there yet." And they immediately get it. It's an effective way to honor them and what they are going through as a team. They can easily understand where they are and where they are heading. Once the team has graduated to the *performing* stage, the fun really starts.

MYERS-BRIGGS TYPE INDICATOR (MBTI)

There are a whole host of avenues that a team can explore together once they are functioning as a unit and trusting each other. Learning opportunities abound in this stage, especially for Millennials to discover that the whole world isn't all about *them*, which is surprisingly a big ah-ha moment for most employees of that generation.

The Myers-Briggs Type Indicator (MBTI) is probably the most famous of the personality tests out there, and it's an excellent tool for teaching active listening and self-awareness. It's also a very useful mechanism for highlighting the value of diversity and recognizing the unique gifts that everyone brings to the team. Essentially, it identifies each individual as one of sixteen different personality types, all of which are perfectly equal. It's amazing how accurate the test results are. Employees love it because it gives such great insight into what makes people tick. Most of them take it home and ask their boyfriends and girlfriends to take it as well. The book *Please Understand Me II: Temperament, Character, Intelligence* by David Keirsey is a great companion to the exercise itself.

Formal MBTI analyses can cost upwards of tens of thousands of dollars per person, and they are typically performed only on senior level executives before and after interventions/training., But anyone can download a streamlined version for free from the Internet. I worked with HR to custom-tailor a program for our department where we were able to teach each of the employees about their personality type for nothing more than our time.

The benefit of these types of exercises in the workplace is immeasurable. One of my favorite outcomes of them is that it gives everyone a new language with which to communicate and better understand each other. Since everyone is new to this, they are all coming at it from the same place, at the same time, and it serves as a real equalizer. All of a sudden, they know the differences between an extrovert and an introvert, a feeler and a sensor, and they can identify the traits in one another with a newfound sense of appreciation. It gives the commune a new vocabulary and a fresh point of reference for their behaviors, which is incredibly powerful and informative. Plus, everyone thinks it's pretty cool they're getting all of this for free as part of their job.

The secret, of course, is that I am investing in every single one of *them*. I am teaching them how to be conscientious team members and showing them how they can do this for themselves. With a little resourcefulness and an Internet connection, I am teaching them how to lead themselves and each other.

YOUTUBE UNIVERSITY

You can learn a ton more about a lot of the concepts and tools in this book by searching for more information online, which is why I have tried to keep this book short and the associated M-stories brief. The more you know, the better.

I first learned about the instructive element of YouTube from an initially shy, quiet, and reserved employee named Jerod. I was interviewing him for a lab assistant position and running through my $500, free time, and what do you do for fun questions when I learned that he liked dog training. Up until that point in the interview, I really had not seen or heard much from Jerod's heart. But when he told me that he liked training dogs for fun, I realized that we were most definitely getting somewhere. Little did Jerod know he was interviewing with a legit dog trainer herself. Before long, he was showing me pictures and videos on his iPhone (of course!) of the three dogs he had trained for his girlfriend while they were in college. I learned that the dogs had all been rescued from the shelter. Hid girlfriend could not keep them where she lived, so Jerod became their caretaker (box checked, Jerod is unquestionably a giver).

Now, back in the day, it would have taken me at least a year of weekly, on-site classes with a professional dog trainer to get my dogs to the level of training that Jerod was able to accomplish with not one, but three, very small dogs (smaller dogs are even more difficult to train). I could not fathom how Jerod accomplished this. I simply had to ask. "How in the world did you find the time to take all three of these dogs to dog training classes while you were going to school and getting decent grades as well?" Without hesitation, Jerod looked at me like I was born during the Dark Ages. He leaned forward, dropped his head ever so slightly, and replied, "Michaela, duh, YouTube!" I just about fell off my office chair. Are you kidding me? And sure enough, Jerod showed me more than I could ever have imagined about learning just about anything on YouTube for free.

While we are speaking about the financial cost of "letting them lead," every single piece of advice in this book is free on YouTube or the Internet. Go give yourself an education and then execute. All that is required is an open mind and a desire to learn. No excuses!

CLIMBING MOUNTAINS TOGETHER

Here's a concept that a lot of people have a hard time getting their heads around: it's okay to care about each other and have fun at work! Most of us are accustomed to thinking that work needs to be serious all the time, but the reality is, when you go to work, you're not going to the library! (Unless you really do actually work *in* a library.) You're going to your commune, or you are boarding your rocket ship, where you are hopefully going to be following your true heart's desire, and you should be psyched about this. You gel with your team, and you're all aligned working toward the same goals. It's good stuff, so it's okay to be happy and celebrate.

Management needs to honor the progress of the commune by offering regular team building exercises and events to strengthen the sense of community and deepen the bonds.

Most of the events that my teams have done to celebrate and team build have been, you guessed it, free! And there's no reason that your team and company can't do the same. You are significantly more likely to get your senior management to approve this idea if you tell them that this is going to cost nothing yet their return on investment is going to be priceless!

Once management is on board and has given everyone permission to have fun and let loose, poll the team and see what they want to do. It needs to be something that is comfortable for everyone (safety first!), thus skydiving and bungee jumping are likely off the table. You have to make sure that everyone feels safe with the decision, which is all just a part honoring each other (and learning to lead). The exercise doesn't have to be over-the-top physical either. Think about having a picnic lunch at a local park, going to see a movie, or volunteering at a local food bank for starters.

One of the best team building experiences in recent memory was when we decided to all go climb a mountain together. Why not? Climb every mountain! We could see the mountain out our laboratory's windows. The whole team was behind this, we made a flag, we climbed the mountain, we unfurled the flag as soon as we made it to the top, we all took selfies, and we all had an amazing time. Some of the people couldn't make it to the top at first, and the more fit of the bunch retreated back down, sat with and supported their teammates, and offered to *carry them to the top*. Now if that doesn't scream team building, what does?

There is no better way to celebrate the commune than by making activities like this a common occurrence. Give everyone a half a day off to go climb a mountain, make pancakes for breakfast, or go to the beach. It's simply a matter of acknowledging how grateful you are to be working with each other.

1 + 1 = 10 RELATIONSHIPS

My expectations are high. I know that. But they are not unrealistic (in my opinion). The relationships that we foster at work are not the average 1 + 1 = 2 relationships. That's boring, and who gets excited about that? Everyone that I employ is a giver; therefore, the relationships are anything but average. They are over the top, psychotically amazing, 1 + 1 = 10 types of relationships. I let everyone know upfront (we cover a lot of territory on day one :)) that I expect them to go beyond the pale for each other and give more of themselves than they have ever considered giving in a workplace environment before.

So, what does 1 + 1 = 10 actually look like? It looks like me suggesting pricey, drab "I'm a Rock Star" stickers, and our procurement guy orders what I asked for but in purple with rocking font and an exclamation point for an amazingly inexpensive price. It looks like one person starting ten samples (instead of his normal, solo two), and then trusting his co-worker to finish them (instead of her normal, solo one). Both employees have to be completely accepting of the fact that on some occasions one person may be bringing significantly more to the table than the other, and that's okay.

There is no drama, there is no resentment, and both parties are equally satisfied with the output, with the full and complete trust that next time, or maybe five times from now, they will complete fifty samples together. This is what trust looks like, and in many ways, this is what caring for each other looks like too.

ROCKING THE COMMUNE

Not too long ago, one of the companies that I worked for asked me to come up with some hard data on employee engagement in the workplace. Employee engagement is becoming a huge management initiative (finally!), and there are some very specific tools that can be used to measure it; most of them can be simply downloaded off the Internet and cost absolutely nothing. Quite frankly, just about anything is measurable, including your personal happiness at work.

The team at this company was in need of a makeover, as they usually are when I get there. I estimated that it would take at best at least one year, more likely two. For whatever reason (likely optimistic thinking), I always tend to underestimate this time frame by a factor of two. My plan was to do a deep dive survey upon my arrival at year zero, year one, and year two with the intention of having three solid data points to share with the board. Don't forget to document how bad (or not) it really is when you first start!

Diligently, I had every single employee complete a Survey Monkey (free) employee engagement questionnaire every year. The questions were really simple—see chapter five for details. The first year (year t = zero) the scores were horrible. They represented what we already knew and could feel; people were miserable. The employees were angry and resentful, they were mistrustful of the organization and of each other, and there were a significant number of toxic, taker employees in the midst. The next year, there was a vast improvement; things were looking up! Then, two years later, I am thrilled and proud to tell you, the scores were positively off the charts. Now, that's what I call a legitimate turn-around.

As you well know by now however, I am moved by more than mere numbers. Scientists know how to manipulate data better than anyone, and I know perfectly well that you can metric anything, including emotions. My mission was to prove *real* improvement, not only in regard to the *what* (the engagement scores) but also to the *how* (the employees' hearts and minds). I wanted to prove that we had achieved a complete transformation, which is a difference that can only come from within their hearts.

The truth is, at the time, I wasn't at all sure how I would prove that the heart of the organization had also done a complete turnaround, but I had unwavering faith that the universe would give me something. This was the same company where I had introduced the SPROUT program, and at the time, not everyone had landed on a special project that they could align their hearts with. Heck, some of the employees were still looking for their hearts!

There was this one employee, Matt, who was a little more

introverted and struggling with "Michaela's heart thing." I knew that if he was going to excel, he needed to find his groove and get into something. It was National Laboratory Awareness month, and I was trying to figure out something cool that we could all do to celebrate. I remembered that when I first interviewed Matt and asked him what he liked to do for fun, he mentioned that he was really into the choreography of dance teams and music. At the time, I couldn't reconcile this in my mind with such a shy guy, but hey, there's something for everyone. Specifically, he was really into hip-hop.

Two wheels in my head started spinning. I thought, how can I align the hip-hop in Matt's heart with the business needs of our organization? How can we get Matt engaged and excited about a special project? Bam! I had it! I approached Matt and laid out my idea. This was right before the Pharrell Williams song "Happy" flew off the charts like lightening. Matt even kind of looked like Pharrell—all that he was missing was the hat. So I said, "Listen, Matt. The company needs something that I think only you can help us out with. It's got to be completely undercover, and it can't cost anything. What do you think about making a video for National Medical Laboratory Awareness month?" He was dumbfounded. Keep in mind that Matt and almost everyone else at this company were ISTJs (on the MBTI); they're NOT sales and marketing people.

I pressed on after he halfway agreed. "Matt, this is going to be great. Think about it. There are almost no rules. The only thing is we need to do is include the vendors, and we need to have it done by a certain date. Beyond that, this is completely your baby. I'll help you round up some people to be involved, but you're 100% in charge."

Matt got totally into it. What he came up with was completely unbelievable. He produced the entire performance in just a few days with his iPhone. He did everything himself, all the shooting and all of the editing and all of the choreography. He told the vendors what he was doing, and they got involved; they hired their own production crew and sent Matt their own video of them dancing around, which Matt spliced into the video he already had of our team dancing, working, laughing and having a blast. Everyone got on board and went completely mental (in a good way) with their participation. When he was done, every single person in the company knew who Matt was. It literally took on a life of its own, and Matt led every single piece of it.

The best part of the whole experience was that Matt had found his heart at work. The video was the turning point in his career. And for me, I had found my proof of the hearts and minds transformation; I could not have asked for a more palpable piece of proof in my wildest dreams. Thank you, universe! Everyone at this company's C-level just about fell off their boardroom chairs when they saw this thing. The video was tangible proof that this team cared for each other and that they were all thrilled to be at work. You just can't fake being happy all while dancing and prancing to Pharrell's hit song with the same name.

After seeing Matt's video, the president and CEO of this company commented, "You know, Michaela, I can only hope that the culture of your department somehow eventually spreads to all of the other departments here." And guess what? That entire company is dancing in Matt's videos every year now!

GIVING LOVE

There was a time when I thought that the *act of giving* was the secret, but over the years, I've come to realize that it's actually a little more than that. The bottom line, for a real return on investment, is giving *love*. The scientific fact is that we are all mammals, and mammals, at the end of the day, simply, genuinely just want (and need) to be loved.

There was an employee of mine whose name was David, and he was a real challenge. The way he came under my direction in and of itself is interesting. I had complained about him to his manager repeatedly because he was harassing my employees. I had been at this company long enough for everyone to have been fully exposed to the Michaela Hart philosophy of life at work. Eventually, David's manager said, "You know what, Michaela? I am sick of you complaining about this guy. You can have him. Take him under your angelic wings and sprinkle your fairy dust all over him. Good luck. We can't wait to see what happens." Great. That's when I learned that sometimes no good deed goes unpunished.

I knew that David might have to go eventually, and there was likely no way that he would ever change. But these things don't happen overnight, especially at huge corporations. It took about a year for me to help him understand that this was not the place for him, and during that time, he made everyone's lives absolutely miserable. He complained about everything under the sun. David would be the one muttering (loudly), "What? We have to go climb a mountain? Are you serious? This is so stupid. We're going to the Harvest Food Bank? What a distraction." For this interminable year of coaching, David begrudgingly and miserably endured our kumbaya-laced culture, complaining all the while to anyone who was within earshot.

The day that David finally "resigned" he said, "You know, Michaela, there's something that I have to tell you. I've been lying to you for the longest time." And then the craziest thing happened; he almost started crying, and with a very soft voice, he confessed, "The whole time I've been complaining about your unorthodox team building exercises, but I want to tell you the honest truth. I have to tell you that I really liked them." Oh my god. Really? He went on to say, "During those activities, you really did touch my heart. It's the only time in my twenty-year career that I felt like my boss genuinely cared about me as a human being. I just thought you should know that's how I really felt, even though I was pretending to hate every minute of it." And there it is.

At the end of the day folks, we're all still mammals in search of an accepting herd; thank you for giving yourself permission to acknowledge this, David.

THANK YOU NOTES

If you could only take one thing with you when you leave a job, what would it be? One of the few things that I carry with me from one place to the next is my pretty, hand-made, girlie box that is filled with thank you notes. I feel so fortunate to have amassed quite a huge collection of them over the years, and I treasure each one of them. When was the last time that you sat down and put pen to paper to thank someone? It's an incredibly meaningful and quickly dying art form, which makes it all the more valuable. Writing a thank you note is a way of giving (appreciation) and sharing the gratitude that is in your heart.

If you can't come up with an appropriate person or reason to write a note, then perhaps you're not surrounding yourself with the right people! How much of a giver are you? When you start giving, it comes back to you many times the original amount. Most of the people I work with have never written a thank you note in their entire lives. I'm a big fan of handwriting, but it doesn't have to be that old school cursive print because it's the thought that counts. How much does this simple (and sometimes random) act of kindness and gratitude cost you? The cost of a single postage stamp—or nothing if you use email!

VALENTINES AND CHOCOLATES TOO!

It should come as no surprise that Valentine's Day is my favorite holiday of the year, given that my last name is "Hart," how big I am on following your heart, loving yourself, and loving those around you. I tell everyone when I get to a new company "Listen, we're not going to celebrate Christmas, or Thanksgiving, or even Easter as a team, but we are going to go all out for the big V day." Oh, you should see the looks that I get, especially from my male employees!

I was listening to the radio in my car on last year's Valentine's Day, and they were interviewing a "renowned management consultant" on "how to survive Valentine's Day at work." His advice included ignoring it completely (this was his number one suggestion), just simply wear something red or pink, and whatever you do, do *not* give Valentine's to anyone at work, ever! How sad that his bottom line message was to essentially pretend that the lovey date wasn't hitting your calendar at all. Now, I totally support the "don't get laid where you get paid" principle (yours truly has forever behaved), but c'mon folks. Really? Just pretend that it isn't February 14th? Uh, no!

Aside from loving the holiday that celebrates love, I also love, and give, Godiva chocolate. Maybe it's because Lady Godiva was famous for riding naked on her horse (I love horses) in an act of defiance for not letting her townspeople lead, or maybe it's just because the chocolate is deliciously amazing. Either way, I love it, and it goes hand-in-hand with Valentine's Day. Everyone on my team knows that Godiva is our official chocolatier and that it's perfectly acceptable to celebrate Valentine's Day in our department. Employees even get Godiva chocolates in their onboarding package!

A few years ago, my team (of their own fruition) organized a cupcake bake-off in honor of our department's favorite holiday. We met in the break room to decorate the cupcakes, and everyone brought something in to contribute: sprinkles, frosting, red hots, candy hearts, cute boxes, little cards, you name it. We had the best time doing this. So much fun, in fact, that other people in the company were noticing. Well, they were jealous actually, but we couldn't stop that. We had intended to share our party with the rest of the company all along; we just had to do the prep work to get ready.

We made a ton of cupcakes that day. We decorated each one and packaged them up in little boxes and then handwrote individualized thank you notes to everyone. As soon as we finished with our decorating party, I sent an email out to the whole company inviting everyone to come and share the cupcakes and to have a Happy Valentine's Day. Of course, all the same people who were grumbling earlier came running in, and we gave them each a cupcake and a thank you note; they were all quite humbly blown away. In this instance, my only contribution was initially giving my employees permission (and a safe environment) to genuinely care about each other on Valentine's Day at work.

I find it interesting that, as a hiring manager, I have probably only received about twenty thank you notes in total after an interview. Remarkably, I recently interviewed a candidate who came to a daylong, multi-person set of interviews with handwritten (in advance, mind you), personalized thank you notes for every single one of her interviewers. I asked her where she had learned to do this, and she mentioned that it was suggested to her in her high school's career counseling class. Now that girl went to a good high school! By the way, I hired every single one of the thank you note writers, including her.

KNOWLEDGE IS POWER

When people are lost, data collection and time can work beautifully together to identify patterns. You can put certain behaviors or feelings into buckets and pay attention to dates and circumstances to start looking for correlations. Data tracking is an excellent way to gather information on yourself and the good work you are doing. In fact, you should be tracking this information somehow anyway.

Back in the day, no one could function without a paper-based day planner. Every year (on Valentine's Day), I would go buy a bunch of red felt-tipped pens, tie a little gold bow around each one, and hand them out to my staff. I'd tell them, "Here is a red pen. For the whole rest of the year, I want you to circle in your day planner every single positive thing that you do. And then, when the time comes for your quarterly review or your annual review, I want you to make sure that everything you circled in red is included in our discussion."

Through this simple action of circling every positive accomplishment in red pen, my staff slowly started to learn that every moment is a choice. Every opportunity is one to reach for the gold ring. And you know what? It's okay to love yourself. Think about it. There's no way that a manager or a boss will have a single clue about all of the amazing things their staff does every day that has a positive impact. This exercise with the red pen teaches people to start *noticing* and *acknowledging* the good things that they do. These days, my staff typically keeps track of their accomplishments in Excel, Word, or on some app on their phone, but the intention and the outcome are the same. Sadly, as mentioned previously, most bosses only remember the negative things that their employees do.

This exercise is about more than just self-love; it's also about sharing the caring. Once they've gotten into the habit of tracking their own positive behaviors and actions, they are encouraged to turn their attentions outward and start tracking their peers. Then, when someone else does something amazing, tell them! Or better yet, send them a thank you note.

Taking the idea of data tracking one step further is the old tried and true manner of recording known to all 6th grade girls as journaling. Journaling can be an extremely valuable tool, especially for those who are not yet ready to go all the way into their hearts and get messy! It helps to give you a better understanding of your intrinsic drivers. Journaling is nothing more than a means of data collecting that allows you to look at yourself from an outside perspective with an analytical mind.

Most people do not actively journal, and those who do tend to give 90% of the page space to negativity: my mother is sick, the dog threw up, the kids were late to school, I got into a fight with my husband, etc. I get it. There's got to be some outlet for the bad stuff that happens, but my challenge to my staff is to start journaling and proactively chose to focus on the positive instead of the negative; get those neurons in your grey matter firing down distinctively different, and positive, paths instead!

LEGALITIES

I know I talk a lot about caring for your co-workers and nurturing the rocket ship, but I want to point out that perceptions haunt this arena as well. You don't want to be perceived as being *too* close or *too* nurturing. Everyone must use a healthy dose of discretion when it comes to creating a family atmosphere in your work environment. There is a very fine line here, especially when it comes to employment law.

I, myself, am guilty of blurring the lines here a little bit more than I would like. For example, when I refer to my staff, I oftentimes casually call them "my kids." This is because I am in a supervisory role, teaching them things. However, the last thing that I want anyone to accuse me of is mothering my staff. In fact, if you ask anyone who has ever worked for me, they would tell you that, regardless of their age, I drive them more like a coach than a parent. Either way, in leadership, it's a slippery slope, and you should be careful to appeal to the lowest common denominator (think uber-sensitive employee here). The lines should not be blurry; they need to be well-defined.

It's easy to take the whole work family analogy a little too far sometimes, and here you run the risk of alienating others or, worse, giving them the wrong impression. I'm sure you've all heard the expression "Oh, he's my work husband" or "Oh, they are work married." Well, we get it, but is that really an appropriate thing to say? What if someone were to get the wrong idea? The first time that I heard either of those expressions, even I, the great lover of caring and expression, was troubled; to be honest, I don't like these terms. Using familiar terms like that can make other people uncomfortable, and if it's unwanted, then you may have a legal issue on your hands.

Here's another one. If someone pinches someone else's behind as a joke, and a third person (think unhappy, disgruntled employee who nobody would ever dream of touching here) sees it and feels uncomfortable as a result, then that third person just might have a legal case. He or she has witnessed something that has made them uncomfortable. It was unwanted to that person in the workplace (i.e., a hostile work environment), even if the person whose behind was pinched didn't mind. You have to be very careful here. I know it gets confusing, but the bottom line is, don't even think about pinching your co-workers behinds, please. And better yet, please let that "work married" lingo go too.

The same applies for getting too friendly or frisky via email. You do not own your corporate emails, typically your company does; they are discoverable by your corporate attorneys with a little bit of assistance from your IT folks. Think *very* carefully about what you put into emails. Imagine reading every single corporate email that you sent plastered on a billboard on the highway for the whole entire world to read. Your corporate emails can and will be used against you. Remember this when you press that send button!

If you are unclear about certain behaviors or have a question, refer to your company's handbook or your state's employment law website for some of the basic do's and don'ts at work. Your company's policy regarding harassment should be very clearly spelled out for you in an easy to find location.

Don't presume that certain behaviors are accepted; even hugging someone could be illegal! Interestingly, *not* commenting on someone's new haircut, lipstick color, etc. was considered offensive when I worked in Europe, but this would not be tolerated in the US. There is no one set of rules, so make sure that you know what they are where you work.

CHAPTER 8

PERCEPTIONS ARE REALITY

WE'VE TALKED A LOT ABOUT THE IMPORTANCE OF focusing on (and loving) yourself. Then we examined the necessity of strengthening the commune. Now, we're going to turn our attention to other people and how you are actually perceived by them. Whether other people's opinions about you are true or not, the court of public opinion always wins in the end. If someone thinks you're a jerk, whether you are or not, you'll be perceived as a jerk. Basically, you *are* a jerk to this person. Unfortunately, it's not up to you. For this reason, it is absolutely critical to not only understand but also to manage (whenever possible) how you are perceived. Unfortunately, being nice isn't always enough!

N = A DANGEROUS 1

The way that I explain this concept is through the scientific formula, $n = 1$. N is the sample size, or for the sake of this example, n is you. You have your own $n = 1$ opinion and perception of yourself. But you don't live in this world all by yourself; in fact, you live on this planet with everybody else, and everybody else is also an $n = 1$. We are all our own separate $n = 1$. Everyone else has an opinion of you; now think about how high that total "n" (or cumulative sample size) really is? You might think that you are fine and perfectly nice, but they might all think otherwise.

Other people's perceptions can be extremely powerful, even dangerous. I was in a situation with an employee one time that became very scary very quickly. I was working in a laboratory that housed infectious disease agents. As is the case in situations that involve highly dangerous specimens, we had very strict protocols in place regarding decontamination. This particular agent could be lethal if it got into your eyes or an open wound.

We had first aid kits located all over the place as a preventative measure, and one of the contents of these kits was bleach. Bleach is not very stable for long periods of time, so it needed to be changed regularly to ensure safety. The bleach was stored in black acrylic boxes to protect it from the light, and one of the boxes in one of the kits had a broken hinge. So, the whole first aid kit needed to be removed from the lab and replaced. Anything that had been in the lab, including the kit, was considered contaminated and needed to be treated accordingly. The kit was contained in double bags, brought to my lab, and stored in a biological safety cabinet with the blowers on, which meant it was in a completely protected environment. Further, one of my employees labeled the box with a huge sign that said, "DO NOT TOUCH! WARNING: This box has not been decontaminated!" He then submitted a work order to have the box repaired. All of the appropriate protocols had been followed.

Then, during lunch, the maintenance guy came in to repair the box. He didn't heed any of the warnings or follow the proper procedure for handling contaminated materials. He ignored everything: the details on the work order, the sign on the lab, and the sign on the box. In the process, he could have contaminated himself. When I saw and understood what had happened, I was worried that we might have a human exposure to the infectious disease.

Now, this is where perceptions spiraled out of control. I called the guy's boss to say that he needed to come to the lab immediately to follow the bleach protocol. His employee needed to stop everything and get down to the lab immediately so that we could assist him. We were dealing with a serious and potentially deadly situation. The guy got an urgent message from his boss to that effect and immediately (incorrectly) assumed that I had called to complain about his work. He found me in the hallway on my way back to my lab and literally put both of his hands around my neck and began choking me. He was so furious that I had allegedly insulted his work that he started to strangle me. He would have likely killed me had I not been able to convince him (between gasps) that I was actually trying to help him and that I was *not* complaining about his work! Obviously, I am fine now, and there were a lot of witnesses and a police report, the whole nine yards. But whoa, really?

Are you kidding me right now?

The point of the story is that you literally never know how your actions are going to be perceived. You also never really know for sure what space your co-workers are in at any given moment and what might set someone off. It's important to consider that every single action will result in a reaction, and you can never be sure what that might be. People can be entirely unpredictable. Here's where trusting or not trusting your co-workers can literally save your life or endanger it.

This was a scary lesson for me, but one that impacts every single interaction I have had at work since. Workplace violence is real. It doesn't matter how nice and considerate you *think* you are behaving; what matters is how others *perceive* your actions. In this case, the guy thought I was threatening his job, and he in turn threatened my life.

TALENT PROFILES

Large companies with deep pockets and vast HR departments have a sophisticated, but sometimes controversial, system of identifying and retaining what's known in management circles as "HIPO," which stands for High-Potential (employee). The idea behind the system and creation of "talent profiles" for staffers is that when a high-level position becomes available, management can look at these profiles and determine who among their existing staff would make a suitable candidate.

The intent of this process is to create a smooth succession

plan, thereby minimizing disruption in a department or organization by already having certain individuals mapped to fill in the gaps. All of this is discussed behind closed doors and most of the mapping is top secret. Additionally, it's highly ineffective. It almost never works because the HIPOs, whether they know they have been mapped as such or not, typically tend to have the wherewithal to discuss their career trajectory with their boss directly and not leave their upward intentions in the hands of secret back room discussions. My point in mentioning this is that *everyone* should be taking care of themselves similarly; why would you leave your upward mobility plans in the hands (or cards) of someone else?

You need to be constantly in touch with how you are perceived by the powers that be in the workplace. Do they see you as a candidate for promotion, or do they already have you pegged as someone who will happily stay in the trenches for the next five, ten, or fifteen years? Most employees are not aware that these "talent profiles" exist, but if you work for a big company, trust me, they do exist in some way, shape, or form. If you're not already having a frank and honest discussion with your boss about your career path and where you are headed, then you need to start the conversation. Do not ever assume that just because you work hard and want to get ahead that you *will*.

If your boss is toxic but he thinks you're a jerk, then you're likely a jerk as far as everyone else is concerned as well. Why? Because your boss is the one with the lead power in this scenario. It doesn't matter that he's toxic. He's the person who is in charge of your herd and your talent card, and what he thinks matters more than what you think.

I have seen people stay at the same company for many years without movement and without really ever understanding why. The talent profiles are highly political, maintained by the top brass, and the HIPOs are traded and bartered like any other commodity. If you're not getting promoted year after year, then you're not on the list buddy! You need to leave. You've been back room blacklisted, and you're never, ever, ever (think Taylor Swift's "We Are Never Ever Getting Back Together" song here) going to get promoted. Don't fool yourself, and most importantly, don't continue to sit there like a bump on a log as the years stream by. Tick tock. Think about the "fit" piece of this. You're not a bad person; it's just a bad fit.

Stop whining and complaining. Accept it for what it is, and bounce. You didn't make the list. Get over it and move on. I know it's hard and scary to leave the herd (commune). You've grown comfortable among your peers, and the unknown next herd can be terrifying. But the sooner you realize that it's just not going to work, the better off you'll be. Speak with your feet and vote for yourself!

My intention is to give the power back to my employees by helping them to understand how some of this high-level corporate stuff works. I see this all the time in the government sector too. You can imagine how political those decisions are! This goes back to chapter one and "nobody loves you, except for you." Start caring for yourself above all. If you have been with a company for two to three years and have laid out a growth plan with your immediate supervisor (including written, progressive job descriptions within the job family) but still aren't seeing any traction, well, this just might be why.

Before we leave the talent profile discussion, why not think about the "untalented profile" pool instead? What about the employees in the organization who should be exited, or minimally, who should be on performance improvement plans? Nobody thinks to have untalented cards or calibration sessions to discuss them. Getting rid of the poor performing employees is the highest return on investment of management, yet we rarely hold our managers accountable for this particular activity. I have led such sessions before, and it quickly highlights who is leading, or not leading, these important efforts in the trenches. Plus, untalented reviews are more entertaining because leaders aren't really sure how badly they should, or should not, present their problem employees to the rest of the leadership team.

THE BITCH CURVE

When you start actively listening to what others have to say while owning your own 50% of the relationships at work, real learning and self-actualization occurs. The people around you are the ones with the power to help you get better and grow professionally as a person. Too much confidence can be a bad thing, especially if you are in a new situation. There has to be a balance between how you project yourself and how others perceive you.

I learned this the hard way, thanks to someone who has his heart firmly attached to his mouth with few filters in between. My lesson was a real eye-opener and one that I was wholly unprepared for at the time. Luckily, it happened when I was fairly young, during one of the very first jobs that I had after completing my undergraduate degree.

This particular department was male-dominated, but everyone was cool with me. So I thought. I was given a department to turn around, and in short order, things unfolded just as I had intended. I had parted ways with the toxic takers, the givers that were left were in a groove, speaking with one voice and performing smoothly, and everyone was happy; I had created an amazing team. The only downside to this situation was that my newly functioning team was intermingled with a department that was not as equally harmonious. It was very easy to point the finger down the hall and say, "Oh my goodness. Those guys are a total disaster. They have a long way to go...." and so on. I usually make a lot of changes quickly, and I was quick to point out the other department's problems without much sugar coating.

When you start to say anything about anyone else in a professional setting, it's a lot like aiming your hand like a gun. You have one finger pointing at them, all the while you have three fingers pointing back at yourself; think about this for a second. I was getting too haughty too fast. I was young and eager, I was riding a recent success, I had my own team, and we were on top of the world. Unfortunately, my good fortune was backfiring on me, only I didn't know it quite yet.

My confidence overshadowed my consideration, and I had no trouble telling other people exactly what I thought they were doing wrong. No one really wants to hear a litany of what they are doing wrong under any circumstances. I was getting way too big for my britches.

The director of the other department had become a close colleague and good friend. He was wary of me at first because I was new, young, and full of lovey-dovey, kumbaya ideas that were contrary to his, but we had come to respect each other and got along quite well. He took me aside one day and drew out on a piece of paper a large, sigmoidal shaped curve and said, "Hey, Michaela, do you know what this?" Of course I knew what it was; it was a classic learning curve.

My colleague said, "No, Michaela. In your case, it's a Bitch Curve." Huh? He didn't stop there; he went on to explain this to me in painstaking detail. "You know, we used to like you. You were fun. You were one of the guys. You were right about what we were doing wrong. But the problem is that you push towards everything that you think we need to fix. You are reaching the point on this curve of diminishing returns, my friend, and your advice and how we perceive you is shifting. You really do have some amazingly cool ideas, and everyone likes you. But too much of a good thing is not good. If you don't stop with this 'holier than thou' attitude, you are going to quickly move from helpful advisor to flat out bitch. You know what I mean, Michaela? Come back down to earth, and you might have a chance of saving this situation."

Ouch. This hurt a lot, but I did know what he meant. I

needed do a self-evaluation and fast. When I did, the situation improved significantly, and I have never forgotten this lesson. And the person who taught me about the Bitch Curve has been on my personal board of directors ever since.

360 DEGREE FEEDBACK

In order to come out on top in this, or any other scenario, I suggest conducting a full-scale, 360 degree evaluation on yourself. It's the perfect way to get a solid read on how you are perceived (from all angles of the organization) and, if necessary, make changes to improve your position. Enlightened people *can choose* to change. Go out there and proactively solicit data on yourself.

Consider who has the most institutional power in your organization. Approach the people who have the most juice, the greatest influence, the richest knowledge, and enroll them in your success. By doing so, you're honoring them, their clout, and their contribution. Flattery *will* get you everywhere, even more so if it's genuine.

A 360 degree evaluation is different from a performance evaluation in that you are actively soliciting the help of *everyone* around you. Enlist all of your co-workers and anyone else that you come into contact with throughout the workday: your boss, your peers, your employees, and a few admins. The more the better!

Make it as easy as humanly possible for them. Hand them a form with your name, department, and supervisor on it and tell them that this will take five to ten minutes minutes tops. It's just like sending a self-addressed stamp envelope in the mail. And you'll be surprised! Everyone will gladly do it. Why? Because people like helping other people. They genuinely enjoy it. You're all on the rocket ship together. And the best part, you can get all the tools and information you need to perform this assessment online for free! I've seen companies pay five figures a person for the same evaluative tools just to fill out the same forms you can find with a simple Google search.

A 360 degree evaluation is the perfect tool to implement when you have a toxic boss or you sense trouble. When all you are hearing at work is the negative from the one guy or gal above you, the 360 degree tool allows you a full perspective from additional colleagues. Your boss can only offer you his or her n = 1 opinion, and if that opinion is less than favorable, then simply use the 360 degree exercise to get yourself some more data.

Stop giving power to the one person who is poisoning you (your boss) and go get yourself a "bonus boss"! Your new bonus boss will love you because you selected him or her. It's sort of like adopting someone as your surrogate parent. You'll naturally gravitate toward a person who is nurturing, encouraging, and supportive of your endeavors. You can approach this person armed with your 360 degree evaluation and say, "You know what, Derek? I'd like to have you on my personal board of directors as my bonus boss." The person will leap at the chance. Who says that you have to let your sole, solid-line manager be your one and only boss at work? Many of us work in global organizations with many stakeholders any way.

I tell people the same thing when they complain about their toxic parents or toxic children. Just because you are biologically related doesn't mean that you have to allow them to be the solitary mother, father, or child figure in your life. If they suck, then simply go out and adopt a better "mother" or "father" for yourself. Why not? The amount of abuse that people will tolerate from toxic people simply because they share similar DNA never ceases to amaze me.

Most people cannot put their own ego on the shelf and genuinely show up for someone else. It's actually been a real challenge for me at some of the companies I've worked for. I will go in and get my department functioning at a high level, weed out the bad toxic people, and create a happy, motivated team of individuals. That in and of itself is the reward. But then, the depressed people from the other departments slump on over and start complaining about their boss or their co-workers. In a very real sense, I become their surrogate boss because I adopt them too; over half of the thank you notes that I have are not from my own direct reports; they are from my "surrogate employees" instead. Oftentimes, a bonus boss is the first appointment to an individual's personal board of directors.

Of course, you need to strike a delicate balance between your bonus boss and your real toxic boss, but it's easier than you think. It's a matter of deciding what to breathe in and absorb and what to leave behind in terms of feedback. But if your real boss is ruining your life, to a degree that even a helpful coach or bonus boss can't help you see your way out of the dark, then maybe it's time to think about speaking with your feet and get out of there. My intention is to share with you a few other solutions *before* it comes to that.

Once again, the entire process that I am sharing with you is absolutely free. That's right. Thanks to the Internet, you can download all of the information and forms that you could possibly ever need to manage your own 360 degree performance evaluation; this exercise adds a nice *how* to the *what* that you are normally evaluated against during performance evaluations as well. This is not an exclusive program designed for big companies with deep pockets. On the contrary; it's for everyone. I am attempting to democratize management and show people how simple and straightforward all of this can be with a little know-how.

It is also possible, in some instances, to turn your enemies at work into your friends. Take a close look at all of the people who gave you negative feedback on your 360 degree survey. Schedule a follow-up meeting with those people and simply say, "Hey, Nancy. Thank you so much for taking the time to fill out my survey and give me your honest opinion. I really value your input, and my intention is to improve and get better. Can you please help me with this? I would like to add you to my personal board of directors and pick your brain on this." If that person says no, the writing is on the wall, and you need to move along. But nine times out of ten, the person will say yes, and you will have turned your relationship with this person completely around.

Along the same lines as the MBTI, there are many additional tools that can be used for this purpose. One of them is a highly useful and powerful analysis called "The Fascination Advantage® Profile"[7] developed by Sally Hogshead. The entire test is centered on how you are perceived and, therefore, how persuasive you are in a work setting. It charts how "fascinating" you are to others and rates what sectors you have the most influence in. Other traditional assessments center on personality types and are built on psychology; they show you how you see the world. This assessment instead shows you how the world sees you and how you can become the best by building on your natural communication advantages. Check it out. I've had a lot of fun with it and gained tremendous insight from this one.

The dean of my business school Barry Posner co-authored a best-selling leadership book titled *The Leadership Challenge*. The core of this book (and the associated workbook) is a 360 degree leadership assessment tool; it's a good one. Even more interesting to me was Barry's follow-up book, *Encouraging the Heart: A Leaders Guide to Recognizing and Rewarding Others*. How sad that Barry had to write a book for leaders that explained to them, in copious detail, how to (or at least try to) care about their employees. Unfortunately, only *"The Leadership Challenge"* went on to become a best-seller. These two books are the only ones that I still have from business school—for good reason. Barry rocks!

---

7   http://www.howtofascinate.com/products-and-pricing/
    fascination-advantage-report

Perceptions are realities in the workplace. The best way to stay ahead of the Bitch Curve is to take a litmus test of yourself on a regular basis. Evaluate the pulse of the people around you and find out where you stand. As the CEO of your company and as part of owning yourself and your behaviors, go out there and solicit data routinely. The real fact of the matter is that you are only 50% who you think you are and 50% who everyone else thinks you are. It's as easy as just asking someone out to lunch and picking their brain. Simply say, "Hi, Judy. I am trying to calibrate myself to the rest of this organization, and I would really appreciate your feedback on my performance." She'll help you, trust me. No one ever even thinks to ask. It's so basic, and it works.

R.E.S.P.E.C.T. – GO, ARETHA!

Shortly after I graduated from business school, I was given an opportunity to lead an international project team in Basel, Switzerland. I found myself rocking my big smile, long hair, and California style in a room full of older Italian, German, Swiss, and British men. They looked at me like I had just landed there from Mars. I forged ahead with my agenda, in spite of the chilly reception, and thought, "I'm not so sure that they taught me how to deal with situations like this in business school." :)

After about twenty minutes of introductions, one of the Italian guys interrupted me and said, "We really don't care what you have to say. We are not going to follow you." Um, what? Aside from being incredibly rude and inconsiderate, he was clearly trying to knock me off my stilettos. Undeterred, I questioned him back and said, "Sir, can you please help me understand what the problem is here?" His rationale took an even stranger turn, and he responded, "Well, it's your pedigree, ma'am. You are the descendent of crazy people, i.e., crazy people who got on ships, most of which sank by the way, and sailed to a new continent to inhabit the new world. We're not going to follow anything that one of the descendants of crazy people has to say." Obviously, I couldn't argue with who the craziest person in the room just might be at that moment; I was dumbfounded. I barely even know who my great-grandparents are (or what countries they had immigrated from), but I did know that I wasn't about to get into any of that with this guy.

Who was he to presume that my parents were descendants of the American immigrants from long ago? How did he know they didn't fly over to the US fifteen years ago in planes from another country? Why wouldn't he view immigrating as an act of bravery or courage instead? Why did my accomplishments and successes account for nothing in this room? Are you kidding me, dude? I was so frustrated, but I didn't let it show. I had walked smack dab into a Command-and-Control, hierarchical, male-dominated environment. His perception of me outweighed the reality; in fact, his perception *was* the reality in that room. To make matters worse, his fellow European cronies were all nodding their heads in agreement with him.

Very calmly, I said, "Perhaps you can help me understand the way things work in this country?" He responded matter of factly, "Basically, we do not respect you. You're going to have to show up with someone more powerful than you before we have anything to do with you, let alone follow your advice or lead." Fine. I said, "Meeting adjourned. I expect to see everyone back here on Monday."

On Monday morning, I showed up with the president of the research division in tow. Without much fanfare and within five minutes, he stood up and said, "We have brought Michaela here as an expat for the next few years to lead this team—based on her success leading teams just like this one at other sites around the world. I don't care what country she is from. You will do what she says, or you will be replaced on this team." From that point forward, my fellow team members were eating out of the palm of my hand. Now, don't get me wrong, this is not the way that I like to do things. But you have to read the culture, and you have to play the game. Perception *is* reality. This was a culture that responded only to the top brass. I was getting nowhere fast without their senior leader's seal of approval; after I had it, my life there was perfectly fine.

ASSUMPTIONS TRUMP TRUTH

I have had the same personal email address for my car racing activities forever. I selected the username when the Internet was first introduced. It's quitedriven@yahoo.com. Whenever anyone receives an email from me, it simply reads "M" in the sender field. I set it up this way on purpose. It's my car racing email address, and I don't want people to know that I'm a girl when I sign up for a race. Talk about assumptions and perceptions!

So the funny thing is, on a number of occasions, this email address landed in the hands of my potential future employers. During one of these instances, I was told, "You know what? The only reason that we picked you out of many other applicants is because of your email address. We figured if you are so driven that you would make it part of your email address, then we just *had* to talk to you." I laughed so hard over this because obviously the being "driven" element has nothing to do with my personal drive. It's simply related to the race track. But they made the assumption, and then it became fact to them.

CHAPTER 9

INTENTIONING

IF THERE'S ONE THING THAT I HAVE SEEN CHANGE more lives at work within the past five years, it's the power of intentioning. Most people don't know what it is or have never heard of it. If they have heard of it, they think it's kind of weird, and they don't really get it. The most common reaction that I get as soon as I start talking about it is "I just don't get it. How does it work?"

WHAT IS IT?

Intentioning is essentially aiming your heart's energy in a specific direction and then letting the universe help see it come to fruition. The hardest thing about intentioning is that you cannot scientifically prove how it works—it just does. You simply need to believe in it and then do it for it to work.

This is a practice that requires patience and cannot be forced. You have to wait for it to happen. For example, if you tell your boss that eventually you would like to be promoted, without even realizing it, you are intentioning. You have put a hope out there into the universe, you have planted a seed in your boss's mind, and it's this single positive thought that can help carry the idea forward.

What most people don't realize is that intentioning works both ways. A lot of people, Debbie Downers in particular, throw a lot of negative energy and ideas into the universe and wonder why they can't ever seem to catch a break. If you only look down to the ground every time you walk outside, how can you complain about not seeing the stars? You're sending all of your energy downwards instead of up and out. It works the same way with intentioning.

Start looking up and opening your heart. Ask yourself, "Where do I want to be tomorrow? When am I going to start voting for myself in a good, healthy, and positive way?" Just asking those questions of yourself internally is intentioning. You are putting your intentions out there and sort of mentally teleporting yourself to the future. It's okay to really go there in your mind with this. Sometimes all that you need to do is turn off the little voice in your head that tells you that this is *not* possible. In fact, the more detailed you can be and the richer your vision, the stronger your chances are of willing it to become a reality. What does tomorrow look like for you? Where will you be? How will your life be different?

There are a bunch of different ways to do this, and everyone goes about it differently. Some people visualize their heart's intentions with physical aids, such as paper and pen. Some people make lists in a notebook or in their phones. Some people create vision boards by cutting out pictures or phrases that inspire them and then pasting them onto boards. Some people tattoo their intentions right into their skin. Why not outfit your cubicle with décor that signifies your intentions at work?

Remember my superwoman song? Interestingly, that song wasn't about my job at the time; instead, it was about the job that I actually have now. When I wrote the song, I didn't even know about the job that I would eventually land. I just knew what I wanted to be doing, so I composed it and sang about it. Weirdly, the job that I have now could not be more perfectly aligned with the intentions that I put out there in that song. I was sending energy into the universe about some things that really mattered to me, and a few weeks later, poof, there I was interviewing for the job that perfectly matched my song. That's how intentioning works!

When I wrote that song, I didn't know that it would actually be recorded, but I did know that I wanted an album cover to go with it. I googled images of superwoman and spent about an hour looking at images online. I picked out one in my head and just thought to myself, "I like that picture the best." About a month later, my team at work gave me a birthday present. It was the exact same photo that I had been staring at a month earlier. I was absolutely speechless. I hadn't told a soul about this particular photo or my song. Now how do you explain something like that? You just have to believe in the power of the universe to align the energy of your intentions.

The same line of intentioning momentum had to do with the city where I currently live. I love this city, and there's a company here that I knew that I eventually wanted to work at some day. I simply told myself, "You know what, Michaela? Life's too short to just sit around wishing for something you don't have. If you want to live in that city and you want that job, then what's stopping you from simply moving there now?" So, I moved there, and all the while I was sending energy out into the universe and essentially convincing myself that the dream job would appear out of the clear blue sky. About eighteen months later, it did.

People sometimes get freaked out because these sorts of things keep happening in my life. They think that I am predicting the future or controlling it in some way. But I am simply actively intentioning all the time, and somehow, someway, the activities or behaviors or life circumstances that I have been thinking about manifest themselves. They may not arrive exactly as I intended them or in precisely the manner that I may have envisioned, but some version appears eventually and feels absolutely as destined.

Essentially this act of intentioning is nothing more than voting for yourself in the future universe. You are removing all of the mental obstacles that ordinarily stand in your way. You block out the noise of that Debbie Downer voice in your head and *dare to dream*. Instead of all that clutter, you focus on the positive, healthy things that would make your life more productive or enjoyable, and you're finally asking for what *you* want. Intentioning is the act of connecting your soul to the universe.

I was speaking to a woman the other day on the phone; she called me because someone told her that she should take a risk and do so (I didn't know her personally). In one sentence, she told me that she was never going to get past the next job interview, and in the next sentence, she told me that she has landed every single job that she has ever interviewed for. I told her, "Well then, it's really pretty simple. You need to stop listening to the Debbie Downer voice in your head and start listening to the Positive Patty voice in your head instead!" Not surprisingly, she landed two job interviews within the next few days. Think about which voice you let predominate in your own head!

A TIME PERSPECTIVE INVENTORY

Are you interested in taking control of your life instead of just letting life happen to you? If you are living in the past, getting a hold on the future can seem (and is) almost insurmountable. From what time perspective (i.e., past, present, or future) are you approaching your day-to-day life? Are you pining for the glory days when you were much younger and everything was bathed in a halcyon coat of perfection?

Wake up and join the rest of us who are attempting to live in the present, as detailed in Eckhart Tolle's acclaimed book titled *The Power of Now*. You cannot control the past. What's done is done. All that we really ever have is this very moment, right?

If you're not entirely clear on where your focus lies, take a time perspective inventory test. There are a number of them out there, but my favorite is called "The Time Paradox."[8] Not surprisingly, a lot of people live in the past. And we wonder why they can't get along with those of us who are always looking ahead! This stuff is fascinating to me because it is so applicable to our everyday lives.

Knowledge is power, so once you figure out where you are, you can make a plan to get to a new place. By attaching your mouth to your heart, you can engage the universe by asking for alignment. And when the student is ready, the teacher appears every single time.

ACCEPTANCE

Occasionally, I encounter employees who are so firmly stuck in the past about a particular professional situation, boss, co-worker, etc. After hearing such an employee mention their Peter Past more than enough times to count, I run them through the following exercise at our next quarterly update meeting. And for the sake of this exercise, let's focus on a toxic ex-boss.

1. I give them a blank piece of paper and ask them to draw a big circle on it. I then ask them to list the attributes/characteristics of a great boss inside the circle. They normally list things like he or she listens to me, he or she provides me with advancement opportunities, etc.

8   http://www.thetimeparadox.com/zimbardo-time-perspective-inventory

2. Next I draw a little stick figure representation of themselves at the edge of the circle.

3. And then I ask them to think about where Peter Past would be drawn on this piece of paper. Most of them point to the very edge or far corner of the paper. One particular employee told me that his Peter Past was on another planet altogether and nowhere close to the paper. Whoa.

4. I then ask them to draw in their Peter Past.

5. I then ask them to draw a rope between their little stick finger arm and their Peter Past's stick figure arm.

6. Next, I ask them to think about all of the things that he did as an employee to try to figuratively pull, or drag, Peter Past into their idealized circle, e.g., conversations that went nowhere, highlighted projects that were never acknowledged, etc.

7. And then I suggest that they consider dropping the rope. Period. Now think about this and breathe into this for a minute. Rationally think and realize that this employee only has two legit options with regards to coping with Peter Past. That is either accept that this is simply the situation at hand (and stop complaining about it) or consider expanding the edges of his or her circle to include Peter Past for who he or she is. This second option is rarely chosen in the moment, but you would be surprised at how often it is precisely where the employee winds up over time; this second option is true acceptance.

Most importantly, this exercise gets the employee to stop talking about his or her Peter Past! This same exercise (separate from the workplace) works wonders for people struggling with acceptance issues about other people in their lives as well, e.g., a parent, friend, etc.

INTENTIONING YOUR FUTURE

Remember the story about my team of rock stars and the business with the mirrors in the labs and the purple rock star stickers? Lady Gaga had her monsters, and I had my rock stars at that company. I gave my team a lot of heat to give themselves rock star high fives every morning in front of those mirrors. Essentially what we were doing was intentioning rock star status for this team, and just a few months later, everywhere we looked was a reference to what rock stars we all were. The signs were glaring. Once you start paying attention, you'll start to see them. Lately, it has been superheroes, specifically superwomen. Go figure!

The secret to all of this is giving yourself permission to let the universe help you. In fact, whenever anyone asks me how to get started with intentioning, I direct them to a book called *The Secret*, which is based on the metaphysical law of attraction. The message and practice of the law of attraction are exactly the same behind intentioning. It comes down to the power of positive thinking and putting good energy out there only to get good things back.

It is very important to remember that there are no coincidences; coincidences do not exist. There is more about the universe that we do *not* know (from a scientific perspective) than what we do know. At some point, many years from now, scientists will likely identify exactly how the metaphysical law of attraction works, but for now, we don't know for certain.

To boil it down to a very simple three-step process, you need to grieve the past, live in the present, and embrace the future! Or, in less kumbaya language, identify your goals, speak to your boss, and put a plan in place. What does your plan look like? Flush out the details and be specific. Remember, the more you give, the more you get! Focus on what you want your future to look like, and the universe will listen.

It's important to enlist others in the process with you, especially at work, because the more people who are focusing on your universal success, the better off you'll be; this ties directly into your personal board of directors. If you have a boss who can put his or her ego on the shelf and have a genuinely $1 + 1 = 10$ conversation with you about you, then you'll be traveling from good to great and great to god in no time flat! Speaking of god, intentioning has a lot in common with praying when you think about it.

There are certain conversations in life that benefit from having a supportive ear. You have to try it to experience it. Once you've experienced it, you'll believe, but trying it comes first. Just do it! The advice in this book is centered on the belief that all of the things that you want and need in life can come directly from you by putting yourself first and showing up for yourself. Forget regrets (from yesterday); every moment (in the present) is a choice.

CHAPTER 10

LET ME LEAD...PLEASE!

MY ASSUMPTION IS THAT ANYONE WHO READS THIS book has an interest in leading, not necessarily other people, but their own lives (this is where it starts, don't forget). I am presuming that my readers want to be in control of their futures and the masters of their own destinies. The Millennial generation employees and beyond are not going to tolerate the old Command-and Control-leadership style anymore. Today's workforce is about self-empowerment. They have access to vast amounts of information, but what they don't have access to is leadership. There are a lot of "sheep" out there and a fair number of wolves (toxic takers), but there are not very many shepherds or sheepdogs! A cute, little, plush, white sheep sits in the back seat of my car and reminds me of this fact every day.

LETTING ME LEAD

I am known as an evangelist for leadership, but even I encounter situations where I am not allowed to lead, where my natural talents and skills are overlooked in favor of more mundane tasks, and where Command-and-Control leadership still rules supremely. I'm telling you. I've been there. I was in this situation a few positions back. I was being paid handsomely (like a ton) for the opportunity, but the person in charge would not let me lead the team one bit. All that I could think to myself was "Are you kidding me right now? You are paying me this much money to essentially *not* lead? Really?"

It was time for a serious talk with myself. I had to get back to basics and remind myself that every moment is a choice. I had to intention my way out of this situation and fast. I could either be miserable about it or make it work, but I knew that this situation was going to require patience and resolve. If what she really wanted from me was a nanosecond by nanosecond email summary update of my day-to-day activities to earn her trust, then that was no problem. I can fire off a slew of emails with the best of intentions. I was going to do whatever it took until she was ready to *let me lead*.

All of a sudden, I had to start following all of the advice laid out in this book myself! She clearly did not trust me, so we started there. I bombarded her with emails that asked her permission to follow my proposed plans of action. I am happy to report that she got really sick of my emails pretty quickly. She tapped out after about a week, and slowly, ever so slowly, she started to loosen her reins on me and let me do my own leadership thing. I had a bird's eye perspective from the Commanded-and-Controlled employee's point of view for just a few weeks, and it made me want to flip the whole establishment on its ear. It was then that I realized that this book was also going to have a "Let Me Lead...Please!" chapter!

Ironically, I was reading L. David Marquette's book *Turn the Ship Around! A True Story of Turning Followers Into Leaders* at the same time that I was intentioning to lead at this new company. No wonder he later went on to write *Turn Your Ship Around! A Workbook for Implementing Intent-based Leadership in Your Organization.* I read his first book and really liked it. It's a lot like this book, without M-power! :)

BUT I REALLY DON'T WANT TO LEAD

As mentioned very briefly in chapter two, it's also perfectly fine if you don't have the intrinsic desire to ever want to lead other people. Some people would argue that this is a wise choice, for at the end of the day, the "delta E," or energy required, to lead other people is a lot greater than simply leading just our own personal self. Leading other people is a lot of work!

I will never forget the first time that this conservation of energy in leading other people concept dawned on me. I was sitting in a therapist's office (this was a really long time ago, by the way :)) listening to a wise, older woman explain to me that the relationship I was in was akin to a fish tank. A fish tank? Really? She went on to explain that I was acting like the keeper of the fish tank, doing a very good job of just about everything required for the perfect fish tank (aka "relationship"), e.g., making sure that the water was the proper pH, the glass was clean, each of the fish were assembled in pairs, the filter was changed regularly, the rocks matched (everything matched, actually), the little bubbles came out of the treasure chest correctly, etc. And she was right; I was taking care of absolutely everything.

Then she asked me where I thought that my partner was with regards to her fish tank analogy, and I wasn't really sure to be honest. To which, she answered, "He is happily back-peddling across the top of the water, my dear!" She was right. He was back-peddling across the top of the water without a care in the world for the fish beneath him being happily paired, getting fed regulatory, or the tank light working properly. And then she asked me who I thought was the smartest, happiest, and/or least exhausted person in the relationship; well, it was him, of course!

While there are a lot of lessons learned in this fish tank story (like "balance" in relationships, for starters), it is a good reminder that leading other people takes a lot more energy than simply doing it alone without a care in the world about anyone, or anything, else.

It's important to remember that leading is a choice. It isn't for everyone, and that's okay! Sheep or shepherd? Sheep or sheepdog? Every moment is a choice.

LEADERS ARE MADE

Leaders are not born; they are *made*. The skill set and mentality must be learned. Not everyone walks into a workplace situation prepared to teach their staff how to lead or even encourage them to do so. In either case, where does one acquire the necessary skills to become an effective leader? How do we teach today's workforce to be the leaders of the future?

My intention, through this book and the simple and affordable strategies that I've been sharing with you, is to show you that leadership lies within all of us, and it all begins with simply leading yourself first. Leadership is something that you have to seek on your own. Fortunately, there are a wide range of legit leadership training opportunities available these days, and it's really just a matter of being resourceful and finding the right ones for you.

It used to take me at least a year, if not two, to teach a new leader how to lead. That time has been cut in half thanks to the Internet. All that I have to do now is simply mention a concept to my new employees, like a personal board of directors or a time perspective inventory, and off they go to YouTube to educate themselves! I have mentioned my favorite books here as well; check them out!

Most bosses are still very much in the Command-and-Control school of thought, which is not particularly conducive to nurturing the next batch of leaders. That's okay. You can go and find what you need on your own. It's perfectly acceptable to simply circumnavigate your boss, if he or she is the old school type, to find the appropriate avenue for yourself. Find pockets of opportunities at your company that will in no way infringe on your boss's power or fall under his or her domain (e.g., the picnic committee, the sailing club, etc.).

Look to your community for leadership training opportunities as well. If you are interested in exploring this area, start small and begin with something that you are truly interested in. Your chances of having a successful experience will be vastly improved if you don't bite off more than you can handle or force yourself into something that you're not interested in. Explore opportunities for leadership at your local homeowners association, your kid's school, your church, your local garden center, the animal shelter, the hospital, or even within your own family. Checkout the meet up groups in your area. Whatever you're looking for is out there.

If you want to learn how to attach your voice to your heart, I highly recommend exploring your local chapter of Toastmasters. This organization is amazing, and it's in almost every town. Additionally, it's very inexpensive to join, and they offer a safe place to either observe and/or hone your skills. It will also add yet another bullet point to your résumé relatively easily.

Leadership offers an opportunity not only to teach others but also to learn so much about yourself. That's one of my favorite perks of the job. But like anything else, it starts with baby steps. I have been astounded recently by how many outlets there are for leadership within the church, no matter what denomination you may (or may not) be. People go to church because they are looking to be led. There is no shortage of volunteer opportunities at church. I can promise you that!

Even if you are in the military, the ultimate embodiment of Command-and-Control, there are ways to lead. Plan a holiday meal for your fellow soldiers or a car wash for your unit's favorite charity. Anytime you have an idea and execute on it, you are leading. Similarly, you can always simply start on you. Just forgo desserts for a week or get back into the gym; even baby steps like this offer you leadership opportunities. It's a chance to gain a small measure of confidence. Tiny small votes for yourself count the most in the grand scheme of things. The number of personal life transformations that I have seen in my employees is amazing, and they make my heart smile every time.

ROCK YOUR STRUGGLE

People still ask me all the time what my story is. We've all got one. Most of the times, something bad has happened in our past. It's just the way life is. You learn the most from the worst. But still, a lot of people don't know how to tell their story or are uncomfortable or ashamed to do so. I don't understand this reluctance. We all have a story, and we've all had struggles, some far more drastic and damaging than others. We are all human beings sharing this earth, and we can and need to share our stories too.

And if you are lucky enough to not have ever experienced a "struggle" of your own before, then by all means, go out and get some experience with people who are struggling. Feed them. Hold their hands. Listen to their stories. Empathy is a beautiful thing to learn.

Our struggle is what makes us who we are. Own it! Embrace it! No one is perfect, and no one expects perfection. Don't use your struggle as an anchor. Use it as a forklift. Use it to get into college, use it to entertain, or use it to motivate. Most importantly, use it to differentiate yourself from the rest of the sheep. Choose to be the shepherd or the sheepdog. Ditch the wolves! Grab or write your fight song. Rock your struggle. Take it to the moon.

MISS THANDA

Have you ever left a job and been worried that you were going to lose the closeness and connection that you had with your co-workers? Of course, we all fear the loss of connection, even in this over-connected society. It stands to reason that our day-to-day relationships have a different dimension than those we keep in touch with here and there.

When I was getting ready to leave the company where most of these stories originated, my employee Thanda (the yang, to my yin, Ambika) took the news that I was leaving the hardest. She was positively devastated; she cried for a few days straight. Her sadness got to the point where we had to have a real talk about it.

I said, "Thanda, can you please help me understand what is at the root of your sadness?" She said it was because I was leaving. She was worried that we wouldn't be in each other's lives anymore. One of my core philosophies in work and life is that we *choose our attitudes*. You know this already, and Thanda knew it too. I challenged her choice to be so sad and said, "We've always talked about bringing solutions to a problem, remember? What solution can you come up with here? Can't we stay connected even though I am leaving this company?" We kept going with this line of questioning, and soon enough, Thanda stopped crying and started thinking.

We soon realized that what Thanda really wanted was to continue working for me. Easy enough, but doing what? I challenged her this time to come up with her own, new job description. She and Ambika had been pestering me about writing a book, but this was the last thing on earth that I had time to do. Thanda's face brightened, and she said, "I've got it. I'll be your literary assistant, and I'll help you write the book!" Voila! And today, that is exactly what she has been doing. Thanda has been involved in many aspects of the book that you now hold in your hands. In fact, I could not have intentioned a truer picture of Thanda's backside with a bullhorn in her hands for the cover of this book if I had taken a picture of her and sent it to the publishers myself!

I love Thanda's story and its outcome. It just goes to show that we are limited only by our own beliefs with regards to what we perceive our problems to be. With a simple shift of one's thinking and a future-focused solution in mind, what once caused tears and misery can lead to an improved opportunity for an even more rewarding outcome. Lemons to lemonade folks.

EPILOGUE

"A leader is best when people barely know she exists. When her work is done, her aim fulfilled, they will say: we did it ourselves."

— LAO TZU

The process of teaching others to lead themselves usually takes about a year. At the end of that time, they sort of graduate from my M-program, and they don't necessarily need me breathing down their necks anymore. They have found their footing and their hearts, and they are in a groove. They "get it." We've been on an amazing journey together, and it's been centered almost entirely around their own personal and professional growth.

They come to a place where they are able to look at themselves as an outsider, which means that they look at me in a different way too. They start to see me more as a peer and less as a boss or a leadership coach. At some point, each and every person I've worked with eventually asks me how I got to be the way that I am. They all want to know where I learned all of this stuff. Who was *my* teacher, and have I always been this way?

Of course, I have my own story just like everyone. The fact is that I discovered my heart, in part, due to my mother's absence; I was very young.

I distinctly remember that I cried every single day for nine months straight during kindergarten. I felt completely engulfed in misery. I had been utterly abandoned by the whole world (except for my saint of a father), and I felt like I didn't have much left at all. And then I flunked. This was at a time when kids just did not flunk kindergarten. I had no idea what to do with myself.

The day that I flunked kindergarten was no different than any other. I cried all the way home and flopped on to my little twin bed sobbing. My favorite Harlequin Great Danes, Kayah and Keyana, jumped up to lick away my tears and see what the fuss was all about. And that's when my life changed forever—right there in that moment.

I said to myself, "You know what, Michaela? This isn't working. I can't trust people. I can't trust institutions. And if I can't trust anyone, then I had better find something that I can trust." And then, right there, I went in (like really far in), and I found my heart. Honestly, from that day forward, I have never looked back. I had every excuse in the world to grow up a completely dysfunctional train wreck of a person, but because I discovered my heart at such a young age, I have been on a selectively upward trajectory ever since. It has never betrayed me.

I told this story to a good friend recently. It never comes out until after I have known someone for a long time; not because I am ashamed or have anything to hide, but because people just assume that I was born this way. This friend of mine said, "You know, Michaela, I've never really thought about it quite like this before, but in many ways, you are a child prodigy with regards to finding your heart." And in that moment, this theory, and my personal life story, made a lot of sense to me.

At the end of the day, what is one of the few things that you take to the grave with you? Your heart! And professionally, what do you take with you? Your reputation! It's not all of the "who said what about who" that matters at all. I know that I was incredibly lucky to find my path at such a young age (and view my mother's role with gratitude, to be honest). It pains me to see people struggling in their day-to-day jobs, which is a huge part of why I choose the jobs that I do. I feel strongly that you should not be permitted to lead others if you are not able to lead yourself *first*. Chapter One: Nobody Cares About You, Except for You; that's the reason that I lead with my heart! Sort that piece of this out for yourself, darling, and you will be M-powered to go! :)

ABOUT THE AUTHOR

MICHAELA HART, once called "*a combination of Katrina 'Kat' Cole and Danica Patrick*", has been a corporate executive for more than 25 years and has leveraged her management experience into that of leader, career coach, speaker, and now author.

Michaela has had a remarkable career in operations, quality, and regulatory roles at companies in the biotechnology, diagnostic, and pharmaceutical sectors, including San Jose Hospital, Syntex, and Roche Palo Alto. She has also worked for a number of Silicon Valley biotechnology start-ups in similar roles, including Vaxart and Veracyte. Michaela is currently the Vice President of Quality Management and Regulatory Affairs for Roche Diagnostics' new Sequencing Unit.

Michaela has an undergraduate degree in Animal Science from UC Davis, a master's degree in Clinical Science from San Francisco State University (with an emphasis in Molecular Virology), and an MBA from Santa Clara University. She is also a licensed Clinical Laboratory Scientist.

Michaela lives and works in Pleasanton, CA. Michaela shares her life with a number of close friends, is immensely proud of her two grown children, Kyle and Nikki, and loves to ride horses, race BMWs, and travel the world.